THE SHOEMAKER'S SON

THE LIFE OF A HOLOCAUST RESISTER

LAURA BETH BAKST

ISBN 9789493231658 (ebook)

ISBN 9789493231641 (paperback)

ISBN 9789493231665 (hardcover)

Publisher: Amsterdam Publishers, The Netherlands

info@amsterdampublishers.com

theshoemakersson.com

The Shoemaker's Son is part of the series Holocaust Survivor True Stories

Copyright © Laura Beth Bakst, 2021

All Rights Reserved. No part of this publication may be reproduced or transmitted in any form or by any means, electronic or mechanical, including photocopy, recording or any other information storage and retrieval system, without prior permission in writing from the publisher.

For Bubby and Poppy

REMARKS BY DAVID BAKST
HOLOCAUST REMEMBRANCE SERVICE, DATE UNKNOWN

The misrepresentation that Jews accepted their annihilation in a passive manner is a historical fallacy that must be done away with. We aim to challenge it by presenting undeniable facts substantiated by eyewitness accounts of those who took part in the uprisings or were close observers of these dramatic events.

We now stand at the crossroads of history. Within a decade or two the eyewitnesses will be gone, and the task of understanding this tragic chapter in history will be left to historians, to those who were not there, and to future researchers who will have to rely on the eyewitness accounts of the participants in the rebellious encounters.

The question that our critics who observed this tragedy from a distance across the ocean keep posing is "why was there so little resistance to so much murder?" Our reply is "look and marvel at how much was accomplished with so little help from the outside world, a world that was indifferent and stood idly by with its arms folded while the Jewish communities of Europe, one after the other, gradually disappeared from the surface of the earth."

In spite of all the obstacles, we know that active resistance took place in many ghettos. Not only in Warsaw but also in Vilna, Bialystok, Kovno, Krakow, and many other communities. Let's be clear about it, the objective of armed struggles was not to attain military victory. This was impossible. The main reason for these revolts was to die with honor. Our choice was simply to die on our feet instead of living a little bit longer on our knees.

Jews rose in successful rebellion. To be blind to all of these facts of extraordinary courage and to accuse Jews of passivity is sheer intellectual callousness. For some unexplainable reason, the Holocaust literature has failed to sufficiently expose the Jewish partisans' heroic deeds. The fact is that Jewish partisans fought bravely in all the territories occupied by Nazi Germany.

Look at some statistics taken from the records of World War II. The Soviet military archives reveal that 500,000 Jews fought within the ranks of the Red Army. 305 rose to the rank of general or admiral. The general record of military history of the Second World War shows that about 1,200,000 Jewish men and women fought within the military units of all Allied Armies, many of them volunteers. It is also estimated that 20,000 to 30,000 Jews fought in the partisans and underground units throughout all occupied territories.

These facts of heroism are undeniable and will stand for time as irrefutable evidence that Jews fought and died courageously to defend the honor of their people, a people who stood isolated and abandoned, while the entire world stood idly by and did pitifully little to stop the slaughter. I challenge those who claim Jews went like sheep to the slaughter or went passively to their deaths.

The young men and women who fought and died in defense of the honor of their people demand of us that we set the record straight once and for all. They have earned their place in history, and we must see to it that justice is done to their glorious achievements.

BAKSZT FAMILY
KEY CHARACTERS

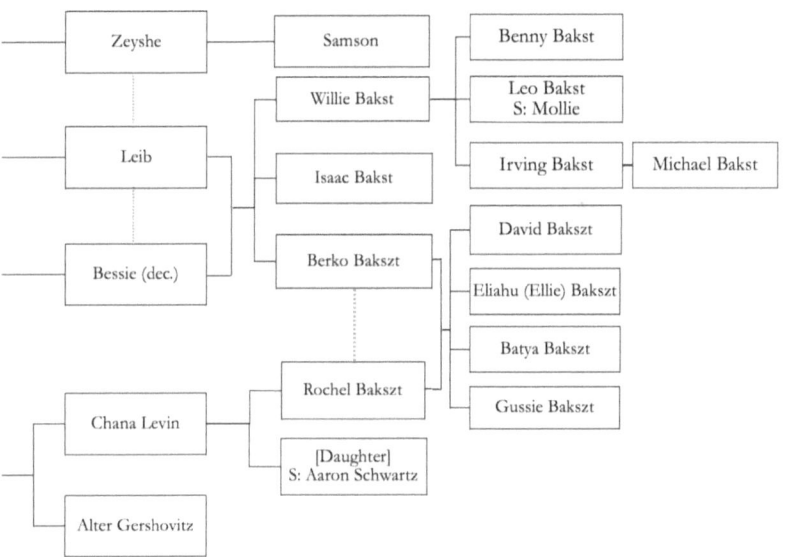

SILBERFARB FAMILY
KEY CHARACTERS

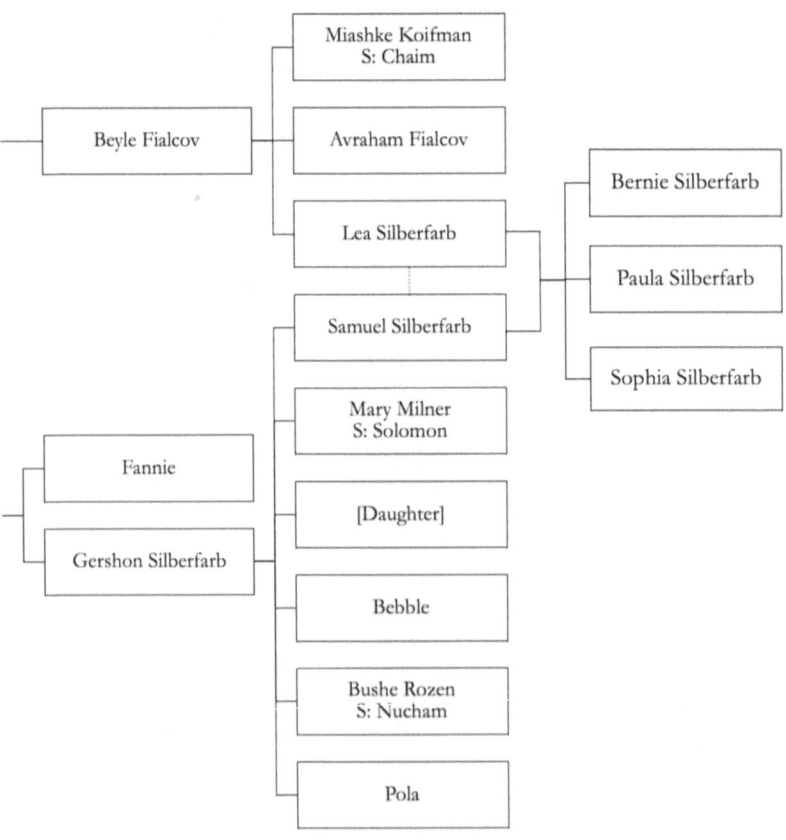

1

Splat. Splat. Splat.

"*Vos iz dos rash?*" Rochel called to Chana, as she searched around the kitchen for the source of the unfamiliar sound.

Chana, focused on her Passover seder preparations, had not noticed any noise. "*Vos rash? Vau iz David?*" she responded.

The two women quickly realized that little David had vanished from the room.

Splat. Splat. Splat.

"*Es es iz vider!*" Hearing the noise again, Rochel begrudgingly abandoned the pot she was stirring to investigate. "*Vas tustu?*" (What are you doing?)

David, with a guilty grin plastered across his face, looked up at his mother as she entered the parlor room. Rochel Bakszt was a burly and warm woman, with dark brown eyes and matching thick hair that caressed her shoulders. She found David seated next to the now-empty pail of eggs that she had purchased earlier that week in the town market. Looking up at the wall decorated with yolks dripping onto the eggshell-laden floor, Rochel could not help but laugh at her son's mischievousness.

The Bakszts lived comfortably. They dwelled on the outskirts of a 4,000-person *shtetl* in Iwje, Poland,[1] roughly eighty-seven kilometers southeast of Vilna and thirty-one kilometers east of Lida. Rebuilt in 1929 due to a fire that had burned most of the village to the ground—the source of which is unknown but believed to have been helped along by some enterprising homeowners looking to collect on insurance policies—Iwje was modern for its day and size, with picturesque brick buildings lining cobblestone streets.

Iwje was heavily organized around its robust Jewish community. Only about a quarter of the town identified as non-Jewish, mainly Catholic farmers living on the outer edges of Iwje. The Jews coalesced in the center of the *shtetl*, which housed three synagogues, three Jewish schools, and a bustling open marketplace surrounded by shops primarily run by Jewish businessmen.

Every Wednesday, locals and merchants flooded the marketplace, filling the central square with the pervasive stench of livestock and the enthusiastic shouts of sellers marketing their products. Carts and horses crowded the frenzied street, carrying necessities like eggs, butter, cheeses, and potatoes for purchase.[2] Women waded through the thick crowd to fill baskets with groceries for the week as cattle dealers haggled with kosher butchers over cows[3] and beggars feasted on breads thanks to the generosity of Rochel and other local Jews.

Outside one of the shops lining the market square hung a hand-painted green sign for "Berko Bakszt's All Leather Shoes." Berko—or Beryl as he was called in Yiddish—had started his own leather shoemaking business in the early twentieth century. The career choice made sense for Berko, who had spent much of his childhood observing his father, a leathermaker, hand tan animal hide. Decades later, Berko's son David spent his early days watching in awe as his father precisely cut large swaths of leather to avoid creating any useless scraps.

The enterprise began small, with just Berko and one employee crafting and selling shoes out of a back room in the Bakszts' snug apartment. Berko met personally with five to eight customers per week, schmoozing as he measured their feet and assessed a price. A few days later, the customers returned to collect their custom-made shoes. Meanwhile, Berko's employee remained perched on a stool, draping leather over wooden forms, sewing it by hand, and affixing the soles with nails. It was a laborious process that yielded at best a single pair of shoes per day.

By the end of the 1920s, Berko's business had outgrown its space. Berko moved his expanding family and factory into an old brick home on Bernardynar Street. After standing for seventy years, the house was well worn by fire and age. Much of the original wood foundation had to be replaced due to rot. The house was situated at the bottom of a hill on the periphery of town, farther away from other Jewish homes and the marketplace, but on a large plot of land near the river that sourced the town's water supply.

Even with the extra space, the home was crowded. It housed Berko, his wife Rochel, their two sons—David born in 1922 and Eliahu, nicknamed Ellie, born in 1924—their daughter Batya, born in 1927, and eventually their youngest daughter Gussie, born in 1932. It also accommodated Berko's factory, which by Gussie's arrival occupied a quarter of the house, employed three shoemakers, and was the only shoe manufacturer in the region to mechanize by importing two foot-powered Singer sewing machines from America.

It was around the time of the move that Berko opened his main-street storefront. The store was a little over a kilometer away from their home, a trek that David and Berko frequently made with bunches of newly minted shoes dangling by the laces from their closed fists. Floor-to-ceiling wooden shelves decorated the shop walls, displaying disheveled stacks of white shoeboxes that mostly obstructed the cracked and paint-peeling walls. On the lid of each box was a picture of a leather ankle boot and Polish text:

Gwarantowane obuwie[4]
<u>BERKO BAKSZT</u>
Iwje

Customers had the option of buying shoes off the shelf and taking them home that day or commissioning a custom pair. The store was open weekdays, closing by early afternoon on Fridays before the town shut down to observe the Sabbath. Local ordinances prevented the operation of businesses on Sundays in Iwje, but Berko frequently came in for a few hours and quietly dealt out the side door with those in the know.

Sundays were generally the only time Berko worked the storefront. During normal business hours, he was kept occupied in the factory, leaving Rochel in charge of the shop. Rochel managed the store on her own with the exception of Wednesdays, when she and a few additional staff struggled to keep up with the frenzy of the weekly market crowd. No matter how well stocked the store was, by Wednesday evenings the shelves would invariably be picked bare.

Rochel's work at the shoe store was far from conventional. She balanced the day job with the responsibilities of being a wife and mother to four kids. In the mornings she fed the children, typically eggs or pancakes, before sending David, Ellie, and Batya off to school and leaving Gussie with Rochel's mother, Chana, and the hired housekeeper. Rochel made certain that the house was fully stocked with food from the marketplace, which she kept cold in the unfinished crawl space underneath the home. On weekends, Rochel handwashed each of the children's two or three school uniforms—plentiful compared to what most children had—and replaced them before their absence was even noticed. Both Rochel and Berko were home for a homemade family dinner each night, a representation of the genuine closeness that they shared with each other and their children.

Two of Berko's brothers, William and Isaac, immigrated to New York before the Great War. They invited Berko to join them, but he declined given his budding professional success in Poland. Berko's two step-brothers and Rochel's entire family remained in town. Every Saturday afternoon after Shabbat services, Rochel would host the full family—siblings, parents, cousins, nieces, and nephews—for lunch. The adults talked politics, sometimes allowing their friendly debates to escalate into harmless arguments, often spurred by Berko's strong Zionist views. The children, meanwhile, spent their afternoon playing outside.

David and Ellie were particularly close. They shared a bed and much of their free time. Ellie had inherited his father's savviness, though he used the skill to less noble ends. He would often play tricks on David, who reciprocated with lighthearted teasing. Each morning by 7:30 a.m. the boys would leave for school together, donning their daily uniforms of navy blue pants and white shirts. Their sister and roommate, Batya, also joined in on this daily ritual. Though the five-year age gap between David and Batya was less conducive to friendship, Batya shared David's love of learning, and as the eldest, David silently looked out for her. This was even truer of David's relationship with Gussie, who at eight years his junior looked up to David with adoration. On stormy nights, Gussie would run to her older brother and curl up in his lap like a frightened puppy dog. David dotingly comforted her. "Don't worry, *Gussienke*," he would say, hugging the little girl. "You've got your brother here. Nothing will happen."

On their walk to the two-story brick schoolhouse located just beyond the marketplace, the Bakszt children inevitably ran into other friends. As a private Tarbut school, it was populated by kindergarten-through-seventh-grade aged children of Zionist-leaning parents. The students came to know each other well, recognizing the same faces from years of weekly synagogue services and Jewish youth group activities.

The Tarbut school students were assigned a classroom, and teachers rotated in and out, giving lessons in their respective secular or religious subjects. Over the course of a single day, David received instruction in Polish, Hebrew, Jewish history, Polish history, arithmetic, geography, and science. Classes ran from eight in the morning until early afternoon, at which time students were released for lunch before resuming afternoon sessions in biblical studies. The school was headed by Principal Novoprutski, who was nice but sufficiently firm to manage the several hundred student school. Principle Novoprutski was also a relative of the Bakszts; he was married to Rochel's cousin, though to David's chagrin the familial connection bore no special treatment for the Bakszt children.

During his midday break, David would often swing by his father's store. He enjoyed the thrill of making a few sales before heading home for lunch. Sometimes he also stopped into his Great Uncle Alter Gershovitz's store for a glass of Lemonado, which came with the added fun of watching Uncle Alter concoct the fizzy drink like some sort of chemist or mad scientist. A man of many trades, Alter spent the bulk of his time making handmade ice cream and flavored sodas that he manufactured for his dozen or so wholesale clients, though he also maintained a healthy base of customers in his basement shop. Outside his business, Alter was active in the Jewish community, serving as a *mohel* during *brit milahs* and *ba'al tekiah*[5] on the High Holidays.[6]

Notwithstanding the rigor, David enjoyed being a student. He was disciplined, spending hours each night on homework after returning home from a full day of classes. His relatively affluent background also made David popular among his thirty classmates. After finishing dinner, David frequently met up with friends for a game of dodgeball or volleyball, particularly in the summertime when the daylight stretched into the night.

In the wintertime, the town lake served as the primary attraction for the Iwje youth. Children rigged up rickety skates by affixing thin metal wires to strips of wood and attaching the contraptions to the bottom of their shoes. This amused David well enough until his father brought him back a real pair of ice skates after a business trip to Vilna.

A few times each year, Berko took a series of trains to the city of Vilna, leaving the Bakszt family to tend to themselves for a couple of days while he shopped around for wholesale leather. Shortly after Berko returned home, a horse and buggy would invariably make its way to Iwje, carrying a load of leather destined to be crafted into loafers. Just as predictable was that Berko would come home bearing presents for his children and the occasional whitefish or salami. The business was time consuming, but Berko adored his family and regularly made time to share words of wisdom with his children or take the boys to synagogue on Saturday mornings. He even made it a point to bring David and Ellie along on one of his business trips, impressing them with the sight of trolley cars in the big city.

Though merely a loving gesture from Berko's perspective, the ice skates he brought David instantly rocketed David to celebrity status among his peers. His envious classmates begged to give them a try, and David enjoyed the attention. David even skated to school on chilly days, gliding down streets that amassed as much as three feet of packed snow and ice.

Aside from walking, the sole means of transportation in the area was horse and buggy, which in winter months traveled on top of the frozen, unplowed streets. Inevitably, there were accidents. When David was five, a coachman lost control of his horse. The horse came barreling down a hill leading into town, the wagon jumping wildly in tow. David was on the sidewalk at the bottom of the hill when he was knocked to the ground in the commotion. Within seconds, the wagon wheels ran over his right-hand ring and pinky fingers. The surrounding townspeople shouted in panic as David lay stunned, examining his bloody, crushed fingers. Berko scooped his son up and ran him to the local doctor. Thanks to several stitches and a makeshift splint, the terrified boy maintained the use of his fingers, though the tip of his ring finger remained permanently curled inwards.

While the streets were not a priority, the local legislature mandated that sidewalks be regularly cleared of snow. This was no small undertaking in a town without snowplows. On cold mornings, men pounded the thick sheets that formed on the sidewalks, sending fragments of ice flying in all directions. They loaded the chunks into a wagon and discarded them in the river near the Bakszt home.

One such winter day, David and his friends were on the lake. After skating for a while, the group sat down, knocking their blades on the thin membrane of ice developing over a large hole that interrupted the otherwise smooth surface. Uncle Alter had the clever idea that he could take ice from the lake in the winter, store it, and sell it to townspeople in the summer. He hired a few local folks to break up an area of ice and load it into a wagon to be hauled away by horse. Alter dumped the ice into a nearly two-story-deep hole in the ground, used a hand pump to hose water on top, and covered the area with a roof-like structure to shield it from the sun. The ice stayed mostly frozen until springtime, when it was smashed into small servings to be used in the drinks that Alter served in his shop and for sale.

As David continued to crack at the fresh ice along the edge of the hole, he suddenly slipped. His skates propelled him feet first into the hole, crashing through what was left of the ice and dragging him underneath the thick layer that caked much of the lake. David smacked the ice ceiling repeatedly, groping around breathlessly until he finally felt the sting of cold air on his hand.

David's head emerged from the water, his body in shock and his heart rate slowed. Through blurred vision he could see his friends leaning over the edge of the hole offering a buoy in the form of a wooden plank. David instinctively grabbed it, propelling his body in the direction of their pulls. Several long and exertive seconds later, David's exhausted body flailed itself onto the solid ice. The boys gave David a few moments to catch his breath before guiding his shaking body off the ice and across the street to his grandmother's house. Chana, horrified by the sight of David soaking wet and shivering, immediately put him in bed and buried the boy under pounds of blankets to combat the hypothermia.

2

Two hundred and sixteen kilometers south of Iwje, little Paula Silberfarb stood on the bank of the Stubla River. Her black hair, bluntly cut at her earlobes with an uneven, thick fringe hovering above her eyebrows, blew wildly in the wind. Paula beamed with pride as the neighborhood children pointed excitedly at the wooden boat about to be launched into the water, the product of her father's labor for the past few months. Her mother, Lea Silberfarb, watched Sophia and Bernie scrupulously, well aware of which of her children would be inclined to make a sudden break for the water.

Unlike her siblings, Paula was inherently obedient and cautious. This was especially true around the river. One summer, the Silberfarb children were swimming in the Stubla when Bernie thought it would be amusing to hold his younger sister's head under the water. Miscalculating how long it would take before Paula started drowning, Bernie might have killed the panicked child had their mother not noticed Paula's desperate yelping and thrashing. Since then, Paula was too traumatized to even broach the water's edge.

Samuel Silberfarb was blind to the growing crowd, busy running around in preparation for the boat's introduction to the water. Though modest in appearance, the boat was a feat for its day, made entirely by hand from trees that had been, until recently, firmly planted in the ground. Samuel and his father Gershon had the boat-making process down to a science. They would buy up a parcel of forest from a farmer in a nearby town and hire workers to cut down the trees, chop the wood into logs, and transport them on horse and buggy to Serniki. Once the logs were delivered to the riverbank, Gershon and Samuel meticulously crafted them into wooden boats with matching oars for use by local farmers traveling to larger cities to sell their produce. Entertainment options in Serniki, Poland[1] were slim—the town lacked electricity and running water—making Samuel's launch days a major local event.

Even so, Serniki's natural resources kept the village's children occupied well enough. The river, used for drinking and washing, doubled as a swimming pool. On rainy days Paula amused herself by stomping barefoot through the unpaved streets, feeling the mud form a suction around her toes with each step. Neighborhood kids played dodgeball and volleyball and inventive games like "cheeseykess," where participants competed to throw a small stick the farthest as measured by a larger stick. The orchard, nicknamed the "Garden of Eden" by Sophia, served as a community park. In the summertime it was fragrant with the smells of blooming cherry, plum, and pear trees and besieged by picnickers camped out on blankets.

Across the street from the Garden of Eden stood the Silberfarb home. The front of the wooden house greeted passersby with a vibrant flower garden that extended around the side of the home. Out back was a larger vegetable garden, from which Lea picked potatoes, tomatoes, and cucumbers for meals. Beyond the vegetable garden, a large wheat field stretched into the horizon. During the summer, Paula watched as hired hands harvested the wheat, which was brought to the local mill to be ground into flour and returned to Lea for use in her baked goods.

Inside the house, the entire Silberfarb family slept in a single bedroom. Lea and Samuel shared a cherry-wood bed, and Paula and Sophia slept in an adjacent double bed on nights when Sophia did not demand the spot between her parents. Bernie had a twin bed to himself. The room also held a large wardrobe that stored the family's clothing, a table pressed up against the wall, and an oak crib. The crib, now empty, had not been used since Sophia came down with the measles and had to be separated from her sister for several days.

On the other side of the interior bedroom wall was the kitchen, with an oversized wood-burning stove that leaked heat into the bedroom. The kitchen held a wooden tub that Lea patiently filled at bath time with water retrieved from the river and heated on the stove in several pots. Once there was enough warmed water to fill the tub, Lea individually bathed each of her children, scrubbing them top to bottom with a washcloth while singing softly in Yiddish.

The dining room overlooked the front yard and was filled by a heavy mahogany table. Against the wall, on the left-hand side, stood a matching hutch, showing off dishes and glasses and holding silverware and tablecloths for Shabbat meals in its drawers. Occasionally Paula noticed the hutch pulled slightly ajar from the wall, revealing a small off-white colored door. Paula knew that she was not to open the door without permission. It connected to a small studio apartment that the Silberfarbs rented to the Neiditz family for extra income. The Neiditzes, with their two children, divided the single space into more private sections with makeshift curtains.

Their elder daughter, Hashke Neiditz, took a particular liking to Paula from an early age. Hashke ran a *cheyda*, a one-room school where neighborhood kids learned Hebrew and biblical studies. When Paula turned three, Hashke began taking the child along with her to class. While most toddlers might have grown fussy sitting quietly all day, Paula soaked up the experience. After just two seasons of informal lessons with Hashke, Paula had to be moved into a more advanced *cheyda*, as the young girl was already reading. On weekends Hashke played the guitar for Paula, asking Paula to guess the name of the song. The one-on-one attention made Paula feel special, a rarity for the proverbial middle child.

Though Paula was timid, she had many friends in Serniki. She was only eighteen months older than her sister Sophia, and the girls shared playmates in the neighborhood. Sol and Chabel, who coincidentally also bore the last name Silberfarb, were Paula and Sophia's ages, respectively. The four children jumped rope and played hopscotch together. Bernie, two years Paula's senior, was uninterested in joining his little sisters but tagged along on visits to neighbors with older siblings.

The Bubrov family lived two houses down. Bernie was friends with the older son, while Paula and Chaiah Bubrov were frequently together. Paula particularly looked forward to when the girls would play at Chaiah's house, impressed by the ornateness of the Bubrovs' daily lifestyle. She admired the pictures of flowers and birds hand painted onto the toy balls that Chaiah mindlessly kicked into the mud. One afternoon Mrs. Bubrov was baking bread and offered to make Paula pancakes with the leftover dough. She served the simple meal on a fine-china plate housed in a special cabinet, making the little girl feel like a queen.

Though less extravagant, Lea was uncompromising when it came to her children's health and nourishment. She baked fresh bread daily from the wheat grown out back, cut up vegetables from the garden, and refused to buy anything but the freshest fruit and meats from the market. Lea served her children milk still warm from the neighbor's cow. She was also adamant about cleanliness, and between cooking, cleaning, and tending to the three children, Lea was constantly moving.

Samuel spent most of his time down by the river working on the boats. Though he was a laborer by trade, one would not know it speaking to him. His face was clean shaven with short brown hair and piercing blue eyes. He played chess with friends and debated politics fervently. Samuel spoke Russian, learned from his days at university in Kiev, and filled the Silberfarb house with books and stories. At night, before putting his children to sleep, Samuel sat on the edge of Paula and Sophia's bed and told them tales of adventures adapted from Jules Verne books.

On Friday evenings, the Silberfarb family shared festive

Shabbat meals. Lea began preparations on Thursday nights, making the challah dough and leaving it to rise overnight. Early Friday mornings, Lea slipped outside to gather wood, chopping it with a hatchet into small enough chips to fuel the oven. She then began the cooking frenzy. Lea rolled out the challah dough on a long wooden board, dividing and braiding it into two loaves before baking. From scratch she made salad, chicken soup with noodles, boiled beef and potatoes, fruit compote, and strudel. Meanwhile, her children were off playing, making their own pretend Shabbat meals complete with "chicken soup" brewed in a water-and-dirt-filled hole. After Lea finished setting the table with a delicate lace tablecloth and her fanciest tableware, she herded her children inside to be washed and clothed for the occasion.

When Samuel returned home from synagogue after nightfall, he would find his family immaculately dressed and ready for dinner. Even after working all day, Lea looked lovely as she lit the Shabbat candles, her black hair hanging long from under her head covering. When she finished saying the blessing, Lea planted a kiss on each of her three children's cheeks. Samuel would then say the blessing over the wine and challah bread, and the family dug into the festive meal.

On Saturday mornings, Samuel sometimes brought his family along with him to services. Serniki was home to a single Jewish temple led by Rabbi Milner. As an Orthodox *shul*, the men and women sat separately. Lea took Paula and Sophia to the second floor, while Samuel and Bernie sat downstairs. Paula, curious as to what was happening in the men's section where she was not permitted, often tried to steal a peek through the small windows that allowed the women to peer down into the male-led service.

After synagogue, the Silberfarbs visited with family. Both Lea and Samuel had relatives in Serniki. Samuel's sister, Pola, lived in a grand house near the town marketplace, which her father, Gershon, moved into after his wife had passed away. On Saturdays, the whole family and much of the Serniki Jewish community gathered in the living room, with its high ceilings, carved stone walls, and views of the marketplace and river. Gershon, abnormally tall compared to the rest of the family, lovingly greeted his granddaughters by hoisting them up into the air as they came running toward him. While the adults sat around a large oak table decorated with intricate carvings of fruit and leaves and covered with trays of tea, breads, and cakes, Gershon gave the giggling girls horsey rides by crawling around the house.

Across from Gershon and Pola lived Gershon's sister, Fannie. Aunt Fannie, as the Silberfarb children called her, had a small store in front of her home where she sold textiles and a large backyard with a garden full of string beans. Not far from Fannie was Lea's brother, Avraham. Lea's widowed mother, Beyle, lived in town with Lea's sister, Miashke, making a living for herself as a healer for locals who believed they had been cursed by the evil eye.

Samuel also had family outside of Poland. Two of his sisters lived in the Soviet Union, one in Moscow and one in Kiev. The sister in Kiev, Bebble, was well-off, married to a Soviet pilot. Bebble periodically sent Samuel packages, mostly clothing for his family, sometimes hand-me-downs from her daughters and others newly purchased. When Bebble and her children came to visit from Kiev, Paula was so dazzled by the gabardine winter dress that her cousin wore that she came to refer to the girl as "the little princess."

Occasionally, Samuel and Lea received letters from Samuel's family in Cuba. His other two sisters—Bushe and Mary—moved to Havana after meeting their husbands in Serniki. They viewed the city as offering a growing Jewish community and greater economic opportunities than their small Polish village.

Paula was deeply loved but suffered as the docile Silberfarb sibling. Lea was kept occupied worrying about Bernie when he missed curfew and snuck away to go diving in the river and keeping her eyes on Sophia. Sophia was less rebellious than Bernie but quite mischievous; she once dumped an entire bucket of sand on a playmate's head, amused that it matched the color of the young girl's blonde locks.

Paula, dutiful about her chores, frequently visited the grocery shop next door to fetch a small bar of chocolate at Lea's bequest. Invariably, Paula would bring the uneaten chocolate and exact change back to her mother, hoping that she might get a piece of chocolate as a reward. Paula watched eagerly as her mother took out three glasses from the cupboard, lining them up on the counter and filing each with equal amounts of warm milk.

Lea then took the chocolate bar and broke it into two halves, handing a little piece to Bernie and a little piece to Sophia. "My pretty little Paula," she would say in Yiddish. "You are a good girl. You don't need any chocolate to drink your milk."

Paula drank her milk, quietly resentful of her siblings' treat.

3

Just five years after the Bakszts' move, it became apparent to Berko that the home in Iwje could no longer accommodate his family and shoe factory. Berko tackled the healthy problem by commissioning a new home to be built on the same property, directly in front of his brick house that he planned to convert fully into a factory. So began a two-year process of Berko assuming architectural management duties on top of running his booming business. He purchased the raw materials, hired laborers, and designed the new home's layout from the ground up.

For David, watching the new house being built was an exciting new hobby that motivated a daily rush home from school. David observed with amazement as the workers delivered logs the size of telephone poles on horse and buggy and manually cut interlocking grooves into each piece of wood with large two-person saws. The foundation of the home was built from a cement-like concoction, a white powdery substance that was left in a hole with water overnight and then mixed with sand until it reached the consistency of farmer's cheese. After the foundation was poured but before it was set, David and his father pressed coins into the cement at each corner of the home, a family tradition for good luck and prosperity. The logs were then stacked horizontally on top of the foundation, linked together at the grooves and separated only by thin layers of grass insulation.

Rochel's brother-in-law, Aaron Schwartz, was a carpenter known for his golden hands. He crafted the home's wooden doors and window moldings, including a small kitchen window that the Bakszts opened for a bit of fresh air in the wintertime. The interior walls and ceiling were covered with narrow strips of wood, roughly one inch wide by two feet long, and then bathed in a plaster-esque material. As was typical of Polish villages in 1935, the home lacked plumbing and running water and was not outfitted with electricity until a few years later. Instead, it contained several tall wood-burning ovens, hand laid from tile and brick, that kept the house warm. On the exterior, the roof was made from gray clay tiles resembling concrete. Berko also planted twenty-eight pear and apple trees around the property, as well as cucumber and potato plants.

When the house was finally ready, the family moved in, carrying their belongings from the old home to the new one. The empty space in both houses was quickly filed. David's maternal grandmother and aunt moved in, leaving fewer rooms than residents. The new home also contained a small office, reserved for Berko's meetings with out-of-town wholesalers and local small business owners for whom Berko placed leather orders in Vilna, as their operations were too small to justify the trip.

The old home, meanwhile, became a full-blown shoe factory. Berko expanded his product line into women's sandals and sold unbranded, wholesale versions of his shoes to smaller shops. At its height, the factory produced more than one hundred pairs of shoes per week and employed forty men of various religions.

Along with a booming business, Berko built a reputation that preceded him. He dealt fairly and honestly with customers and employees, developing relationships not only within the tight-knit Jewish community in Iwje but also with Catholic Poles. Customers from up to one hundred kilometers away made the trek by wagon to fit their feet in a pair of Berko Bakszt's shoes, and Iwjeans paid as much as twice the price of competitor products for the higher-quality alternative. Berko was doing double the business of the seven other shoes stores in town combined.

Though Berko's connections helped, like all Jews in Iwje, the Bakszts were not immune from antisemitism. Many non-Jewish children in Iwje befriended their Jewish counterparts in the town's public school; others threw rocks at David and Ellie. The Bakszt boys generally followed their parents' instructions to ignore the harassment, but the encounters occasionally escalated into fist fights.

Jewish businesses were taxed more heavily by the local assessor, sometimes forcing small, family-run shops into bankruptcy. Berko's non-Jewish associates gave him advance warning of when the tax assessor was coming to town, providing Berko with an opportunity to move most of the inventory off the store's shelves and into a narrow cellar hidden below the floorboards. The apparently reduced shoe stock combined with the few dollars that Berko quietly passed to the official usually left him with a bill that somewhat resembled what he actually should have been charged.

Berko and Rochel tried to reassure their children that they were safe in Iwje, but stories of attacks on Jews were commonplace. The young Jewish men in Iwje often assumed responsibility for protecting their people. Sometimes the assaults were isolated. When a group of Polish farmers walked through town on their way to church, one stopped to yank on the beard of an elderly Jewish man sitting on a porch. The Jewish youth beat the farmer in retaliation, stuffing him into an outhouse.

Other threats were more serious. An antisemitic political party was gaining traction in Poland and inching its way toward Iwje. The far-right group infiltrated other towns, marching in the streets with banners calling for boycotts of Jewish businesses. With the tacit consent of the police, the group organized pogroms that burnt down Jewish stores, threw rocks through the windows of Jewish homes, and chased, beat, and even killed Jewish men. Iwje's young men and Jewish-run fire department began preparing for a physical resistance. Ultimately, their mobilization deterred the interlopers.

Notwithstanding David's cognizance of growing tension and the possibility that he may one day need to defend his *shtetl*, his world remained stable as he entered his teenage years. David had a budding social life, filling evenings by walking around town with classmates and attending Jewish youth group meetings. The summer before his sixteenth birthday, in 1938, David met Macha Kameneski, a Jewish girl who lived in the nearby city of Nowogrodek. Macha spent her summers in Iwje, staying with extended family who resided across the street from David's Uncle Alter. David and Macha quickly became infatuated with one another, spending the summer months together and passing winter months writing letters back and forth.

During that same period, Jews in Germany were living under increasingly hostile Nazi rule, bound by hundreds of restrictions that turned them into second-class citizens. By 1934, Jews in Germany were excluded from civil service, subjected to stringent quotas for attendance at schools and universities, and restricted in their ability to practice law, medicine and accounting.[1] In September 1935, the *Reichstag* (German parliament) passed the infamous Nuremberg Laws, which, finding inspiration in America's racist Jim Crow laws, served as the basis for Germany's Aryan race regime.[2] The Reich Citizenship Law, as amended in November 1935, stripped Jews of their German citizenship, the right to vote, and the ability to occupy public office.[3] The Law for the Protection of German Blood and German Honor criminalized marriages and sexual relationships between Jews and German citizens as well as forbade Jews from displaying the German flag or national colors.[4] Though Germany briefly tempered its persecutions in the lead up to the 1936 Berlin Olympics, it continued to disenfranchise Jews by seizing their businesses and dismissing Jewish workers.[5] In 1938, The Executive Order on the Law on the Alteration of Family and Personal Names required that Jews in Germany bearing "non-Jewish" first names add "Israel" or "Sara" to their names, and Jews were forced to carry identification cards and have their passports stamped with a red "J."[6]

The fall after Macha returned home, escalating violence in Germany finally reached Poland's borders. Once Germany annexed

Austria, the Polish government sought to denationalize certain Polish citizens living abroad, fearing an influx of Austrian Jews who held Polish passports and endeavored to flee the antisemitic regime. The Germans were equally unkeen on keeping the Polish Jews within their territory and sent the Gestapo (the Nazi secret police) to forcibly deport them in late October 1938. Approximately 17,000 Jews with Polish citizenship were dragged from their homes —often beds—and placed in temporary detention camps. The prisoners, including women, children, and the elderly, were then crammed into trucks and trains and marched to the Polish border as people flooded the streets screaming, "*Juden raus* to Palestine!" (Jews out to Palestine!).[7] Many deportees died from illness, exhaustion, and suicide.

The situation culminated in a confrontation at the German-Poland border, where Jews were directed back and forth by German and Polish guards in a game of human ping-pong. Though some Jews were initially let into Poland, thousands remained stateless in the no man's land between the two sovereigns. The Red Cross and Jewish charities provided aid, but the refugees lived in overcrowded and dirty conditions, lacking basic food, clothing, medicine, and shelter. Some desperate refugees attempted to escape back into Germany, the unsuccessful of whom were shot.

By November 1938, as winter weather worsened conditions for the refugees, news of this *Polenaktion* spread through Europe. Herschel Grynszpan, a teenage Jew whose parents emigrated from Poland to Germany, was living in France when he received news that his parents and siblings were among the refugees trapped at the border. Four days later, Grynszpan shot a German embassy official in Paris in an alleged act of vengeance. German Propaganda Minister Joseph Goebbels used the incident as political capital. He gave an incendiary speech suggesting that the "World Jewry" had conspired to carry out the assignation and any retaliatory demonstrations against Jews would not be quashed by the police.

So began *Kristallnacht*. Over two days, pogroms across Germany looted and vandalized thousands of Jewish businesses and homes. Synagogues were burned to the ground, with local authorities intervening only to prevent the fires from threatening other buildings. Jewish cemeteries were desecrated. Jews were assaulted, raped, arrested, and murdered.

News spread to Iwje. The paper delivered to the Bakszts' home featured stories of the riots. Radios were far from ubiquitous, but Berko's non-Jewish neighbor happened to own one, and Berko frequently stopped by to listen in on the daily broadcast. The Bakszts were horrified by the stories; far from the German border, life in Iwje still seemed ordinary.

Shortly thereafter, Rochel fell ill. She had heavy vaginal bleeding, extreme weakness, and a bloated, pregnant-like stomach. To combat the resultant anemia, Batya ground up chicken livers and fed them to her mother with a spoon. Berko took Rochel to Vilna to see a doctor who concluded that Rochel had an incurable stomach tumor. She was hospitalized, leaving her husband traveling back and forth between Vilna and Iwje to tend to her, their children, and the business.

Rochel stayed in Vilna for months, her condition deteriorating. At one point, she became so weak that she could not talk or eat. Nurses squeezed oranges into her mouth in an attempt to keep her nourished. Rochel's children, meanwhile, remained in school in Iwje. Separated from her for an extended time and without any answers, they grew increasingly worried about her wellbeing. After the two teenagers finished their spring exams, David and Ellie took the train to Vilna to visit their ailing mother. Berko warned his sons that Rochel was unlikely to make it much longer.

David and Ellie pulled up in a horse and buggy where they spotted Rochel waiting eagerly in the window. She was a shell of herself, frail and sluggish. As if moving in slow motion, Rochel gradually stretched out her hands to grasp them, her face tired but gleaming with excitement. "*Dovidke*," she called David. "Look how tall you are! And look how nice *Ellieke* looks!" She squeezed the now young men as tight as she could. David was shocked to feel how weak his mother had grown.

Rochel eventually expelled a mass from her body. Though the tissue did not resemble a fetus and she was told that she was not pregnant, Rochel described the experience as akin to labor. Almost immediately, she felt well again. The doctors were perplexed and unable to render a diagnosis. They said it was a miracle that she had survived.

By the end of summer 1939, David was a happy young man. His mother had returned home and regained her health. He had been accepted to business school, and his brother was college bound. And, David had spent the prior few months savoring Macha's company.

On September 1, 1939, Germany invaded Western Poland. Two days later, Britain and France declared war on Germany, signifying the beginning of World War II. Unbeknownst to the Western powers, the Molotov–Ribbentrop non-aggression pact signed just a week earlier between Germany and the Soviet Union contained a secret protocol for the division of Eastern Europe between the two nations. They agreed to partition Poland, with the western half falling to Germany and the eastern half to the Soviet Union. Joseph Stalin invaded Poland from the east on September 17, 1939.

PHOTOS

Standing left to right: Ellie Bakszt, Rochel Bakszt, David Bakszt. Seated left to right: Batya Bakszt, Berko Bakszt. Iwje, Poland, 1929 or 1930.

Gussie Bakszt (third from left) and three cousins in Iwje, Poland, 1938.

Ellie Bakszt in a school picture in Iwje, Poland, 1939.

Rochel Bakszt's extended family. Farthest left: David Bakszt. Back row standing (behind David), left to right: Berko Bakszt, Rochel Bakszt, Ellie Bakszt. Seated next to (slightly front of) David: Chana Levin. Seated front row, farthest left: Batya Bakszt. Iwje, Poland, 1939.

David Bakszt in his father's shoe store in Iwje, Poland, 1938 or 1939.

David Bakszt and Macha Kameneski in Iwje, Poland, date unknown.

Left to right: Sophia Silberfarb and Paula Silberfarb in Gershon Silberfarb's backyard. Serniki, Poland, 1938.

Samuel Silberfarb in Serniki, Poland, date unknown.

Gershon Silberfarb, location and date unknown.

Lea Silberfarb in Serniki, Poland, date unknown.

4

Like an ant infestation, the Red Army appeared in Iwje a few at a time and then suddenly all at once. As the first Soviet soldiers materialized, so too did the rumors of an impending invasion. Roughly one week later, tanks flooded the streets. Unequipped for a military attack and with much of Polish leadership preoccupied fighting the Germans in the west, Iwje quickly succumbed to the Soviet aggressors.

The initial response to the arrival was mixed. Most Poles opposed the occupation, driven primarily by nationalist sentiments. Jews, many of whom were comfortably middle class, feared what Soviet rule would mean for their trades. But others were more sympathetic to Soviet communism. They viewed it as an opportunity for greater prosperity in a society unencumbered by antisemitism.

Almost immediately, the Soviet Union communized and Sovietized Iwje. It disbanded religious and political organizations and seized control of the media. The Soviets withdrew the Polish złoty from currency without warning, costing Iwjeans their entire livelihoods in the process. Those who paid the steepest price were the local, generally Jewish, capitalists, who lost their businesses and properties.

The Soviets approached Berko as he was entering his shoe factory one morning. "Where do you think you're going?" one soldier asked him.

"This is my factory," Berko answered, gesturing at the building.

The soldier held out his hand, demanding the keys to the building. "Yes, it's your factory," he responded. "It's your factory, it's my factory, it's his factory." The soldier pointed to a man walking on the other side of the street. "It's everybody's factory. Everything belongs to you now."

In reality, nothing belonged to him. Berko became a poor man overnight.

Initially, the Soviets allowed Berko to continue managing the factory, as they lacked a suitable alternative. Even so, the Bakszt family's lives were hard. The pay was next to nothing and runs on necessities meant that Rochel had to wait in line all day for just a piece of bread. As one of the only businessmen in Iwje who employed several laborers, Berko was targeted by the Soviets as an "exploiter." They took over the family home, forcing the Bakszts to quarter a Soviet lieutenant and captain.

Several times each week, the Soviets dragged Berko from his bed in the dead of night, taking him to an NKVD outpost to be tortured with extensive questioning and sleep deprivation. The NKVD, a Soviet secret police force and precursor agency to the KGB, asked Berko endlessly about his former shoe business, demanding information about his inventory, employees, and their compensation. Regardless of what early morning hour Berko was eventually returned home, he was nonetheless expected to drag his exhausted body into the factory at his regular start time.

While Berko tried to minimize the impact on his family, the Bakszts lived in constant fear. Rochel rarely slept, terrified that the NKVD would barge in at any moment. On nights when Berko was interrogated, she sat anxious by the front window praying that her husband would be returned home unscathed by dawn. Even neighbors, assumed to be affiliates of Berko, were hauled in for interviews about the shoe factory. One neighbor told Berko that he had tried to help by denying any knowledge of the business or Bakszt family, an obvious lie that only made matters worse.

Though they understood less than their parents, the Bakszt children could sense the terror. The streets were intimidating, occupied by military trucks and tanks where, just months prior, no automobile had ever been. The children were menaced by Soviet officials, who, armed with guns, uniforms, and stern looks, might stop them at any time. All of the Bakszts were kept awake at night by stories of capitalist families and local Jewish leaders who were snatched from their beds and deported to Siberia or Gulag labor camps, never to be seen again. Berko and Rochel often sent their children to sleep at an aunt or uncle's home, hoping that if the Soviets came to transport the family, their children would be spared. On such nights, David, Ellie, Batya, and Gussie worried that come morning, they would be returning to a home inhabited only by Soviets.

The Soviets issued the Bakszt children new passports, stained with an undesirable stamp indicating that they were descendants of a capitalist. Their Tarbut school was converted into a Soviet school that they were required to attend, even on the Sabbath. They were no longer permitted to speak in Hebrew or undertake any religious studies; the curriculum instead taught Russian and preached communism and allegiance to the Motherland.

David, Ellie, Batya, and Gussie became outcasts, bullied and abandoned by those who had previously been considered friends. Some of their less-affluent peers supported communism, which promised access to a higher education system that historically capped Jewish enrollment. David could no longer work in the shoe store during lunch, so he passed the time studying. On the rare occasion when he was invited out with other teenagers he declined, feeling too guilty having fun while his parents suffered. David's only solace was the occasional letter he received from Macha.

After about nine months, the Soviets dissolved Berko's factory, sending his remaining inventory and capital to Russia. Berko was unemployed and unemployable. Nobody wanted to hire a former businessman. Having hidden some of his leather shoes under the floorboards in his house, Berko was able to trade them for basic supplies from local farmers to keep his family from starving. Rochel found creative ways to purpose whatever food Berko scrounged up into meals, mostly potatoes, wheat, and milk from a cow that they kept in a small barn adjacent to the house.

Berko eventually found a job cutting down trees in the woods. It was physically taxing work, particularly for a man in his early forties with a hernia, but Berko considered himself lucky to no longer be among the many unemployed. Like everyone who had a job in Iwje, he worked long days for insufficient pay. Meanwhile, the children chipped in where they could, helping fetch water from the river and wood from the forest.

Though Berko and Rochel made efforts to quietly maintain their Jewish faith, it was difficult. Berko worked on the Sabbath and holidays, and the children were in school. The town's main synagogue was converted into a grain storage facility, and the mere use of Hebrew risked Soviet persecution. Ellie, David, and Batya's Jewish youth group was dissolved. The once tight-knit Jewish community had little time for even secular socializing, as daily life revolved around searching for necessities.

As life grew increasingly miserable under the Soviets, so did the news about the Nazi invasion in Western Poland. The Germans were rumored to be confiscating property from Jews and forcing them into ghettos and labor camps. Stories percolated of Hitler's continued expansion across Europe, with incursions in Denmark, Norway, the Netherlands, Belgium, Luxembourg, and France. Berko understood that the Germans were a threat—he had fought with the Red Army against them during World War I—but it was also hard to imagine that living under German rule could possibly be worse than life under Soviet control.

After more than a year and a half of Soviet rule in Eastern Poland, Hitler breached his non-aggression pact with Stalin and attacked the Soviet Union on June 22, 1941. Iwje was located only a couple hundred kilometers from the front. Within days, the *Luftwaffe*, or German Air Force, conducted three air raids over Iwje.

The Germans dropped bombs that flattened buildings and burned entire streets.

The Bakszts stayed hidden in their home, listening as the distant blasts grew deafening. The earth-shattering bangs scared Gussie, and the awareness that their home—with them in it—may soon be reduced to a pile of charred wood panicked the rest of the family. Rochel, Berko, and Chana tried to remain calm for the sake of the children, but everyone was trembling. One blast demolished Alter's empty shop. Others came within mere blocks of the Bakszsts' home, violently shaking the house and filling the air with heavy dust and smoke.

The bombings scared off most of the Red Army before the German Army had even set its leather boots on the ground in Iwje. Many Jews fled to neighboring villages, seeking to outrun the apparently imminent Nazi arrival. Others stayed put, hidden in cellars and attics as local non-Jews, temporarily liberated from the restrictions of governance, looted formerly Jewish businesses and homes.

Nazi soldiers swarmed the streets of Iwje on June 30, 1941. They focused first on chasing away what remained of the Soviet forces. The Bakszts, like all Jews in Iwje, kept inside their home, avoiding the German soldiers. Many non-Jewish Poles, still averse to foreign occupation, did the same. Others greeted the Nazis with open arms, either because they agreed with their fascist policies or simply saw it as a superior alternative to communism.

The Soviets quickly disappeared, and the Nazis turned their full attention to the Jews. They ordered all Jews to report to the marketplace for registration. Thousands of people assembled. The Jews were told that they were required to wear a yellow Star of David labeled "*Jude*" on the front and back of their clothing at all times. Jewish wives across town tore up pieces of yellow fabric—made from scraps of existing clothing or linens—into six-point stars and sewed or pinned them onto their families' clothing.

All Jewish men ages sixteen to sixty were put to work.[1] The fortunate cleaned streets or polished German cannons. Hundreds at a time strained to drag away abandoned Soviet tanks using cable wires. David and Ellie spent their days on their hands and knees in the hot sun, pulling out the grass that grew between the sidewalk stones and sweeping them clean. The Nazis were perched on every street and every corner, hovering over the workers on foot or from horseback. Older Jews who were too frail for physical labor were shot in place, the piercing sound of gunshots sending a chilling warning to the remaining Jews of what would happen if they did not obey orders. Those who paused for a break or worked too slowly were beat with the rubber whips that the Nazis used to control their horses.

One day, David was startled by the stinging crack of the whip on his back as he mimicked the gesture of picking grass, desperate to give his body a short reprieve. The pain was sharp and paralyzing, and he struggled to keep himself from crying out. David forced himself to muster the strength to continue slaving away; the only alternative to German torture was to meet the fate of those who could not keep up.

Under Nazi rule, Jewish families were not only exhausted but also starved and dehydrated. They were required to physically labor seven days a week, from dawn to dusk, receiving no money and only a single slice of bread at the end of each day. Meanwhile, the Catholic Poles carried on with their daily lives. Some were adopted by the Germans into a local police force. Others remained farmers, tending to agriculture and livestock on the edges of town.

Berko occasionally snuck away before dawn to meet with local Polish farmers he had befriended during his shoemaking days. The farmers offered Berko food for his family and information about Nazi plans, sometimes out of pity and sometimes in exchange for a pair of shoes that Berko had kept hidden. They warned him that the Germans had set up mobile killing squads, the *Einsatzgruppen*, that trailed the Germany army and carried out mass murders in newly occupied territories. The shootings had recently plagued nearby towns, and it was only a matter of time before the *Einsatzgruppen* made its way to Iwje.

Believing these claims, Berko warned his family that under no circumstances were they ever to report should the Nazis summon the Jews to assemble. "Find a way, hide, but you get yourselves as far away as possible," he told them. Berko gave the family specific instructions on locations to seek shelter based on where they might be at the time of a German order. By the time the conversation finished, he had mapped out hiding places across the town.

Life continued this way until August 2, 1941, or *Tisha B'Av*, the ninth of the Jewish month of Av. The saddest day of the Jewish calendar, many Jews were fasting to commemorate the destruction of the two holy Temples in Jerusalem and other historical massacres, including prior expulsions of the Jewish people from Europe. Berko rose early that morning to visit with a Polish farmer. Not long after his departure, a truck rolled into town carrying several Gestapo officers. The roar of its engine, still a jarring sound in the once-quiet town, was immediately noticed by the Jewish locals.

The Gestapo demanded that Jewish men gather immediately in the market, sending out several local officers and Jews to disseminate the news. They ran around the town pounding on doors and shouting for Jews to report. The streets quickly devolved into chaos, with wives and mothers watching hysterically as their loved ones were torn away.

Farther out, the Bakszt family was still home, except for Berko. Hearing the shouting in the distance, David demanded that his mother, grandmother, aunt, and siblings all hide. They quietly made their way out of the house and into their small barn—one of the predetermined hiding places. Most of the space was occupied by the cow. But above their heads hung a single lofted shelf used to store extra hay with a wooden ladder propped up against it. One by one, they climbed up the ladder and hoisted themselves over the hay bales. Shielded in the narrow space between the barn walls on three sides and the hay lining the open interior edge of the shelf, the Bakszts packed themselves tightly together and pressed their bodies flat against the wood.

The family lay quiet, listening to the sounds of their rapidly beating hearts and muffled shouting in the streets. After several seemingly year-long minutes, David lifted his head and peered out a small window that overlooked Bernardynar Street. He saw German police traveling door-to-door, ushering Jews in the direction of the market. Three soldiers were approaching the barn.

David slammed his head back down. A few moments later, the barn door creaked open filling the space with sunlight. Three Nazis entered, accompanied by a large dog that began frantically barking. Peeking through the wooden planks below his head, David could see a large German Shepard standing on its hind legs and looking up directly at him. Without even realizing it, David was holding his breath, too afraid to make even the slightest of movements. After peering around the barn for a few seconds, one of the Germans snapped at the dog. "Come on, leave that smell. Let's get out of here!" David realized that the Nazis thought that the dog was reacting to the stench of the cow.

Even after the soldiers had left and the barn had grown dark, the family did not dare move. They stayed hidden on the shelf for hours, hungry, hot, and worried about the fate that had befallen Berko and their community.

Shortly after nightfall, Berko entered the barn. "Are you up there?" he asked softly.

"Yes," David answered.

"Okay, you can come down now," Berko said, helping his family down the ladder.

Berko, who had been in the non-Jewish area of Iwje, was able to hide with a Polish farmer to avoid the roundup. Meanwhile, the Nazis gathered the male Jews in the marketplace, lining them up in rows where they stood baking in the sun for hours and uncertain of their fates.

The Germans first commanded the rabbis to step forward, instructing one to throw his prayer book on the ground. When he refused, the rabbi was beaten in front of his congregants.[2] After the religious figures were identified, the Germans, with the help of the local Polish police force, combed through more than 1,000 Jews, pulling out of line those known to have held leadership roles in the community. Some Iwjeans lied about their professions when asked, claiming to practice in trades they presumed more useful to the

Nazis. Many were caught in their mistruths by the Polish helpers who recognized their once-fellow citizens and were beaten or killed on the spot. Principal Novoprutski fell into this unlucky group and was repeatedly beat over the head with a piece of metal by one of the local police.[3]

The selected townspeople—mainly teachers, businessmen, and religious figures—were loaded into trucks and driven away in batches. For most of the Jews, it was their first time in a motor vehicle, their panic exacerbated by the unfamiliar roar of the engine. Hoarded into the cargo beds, the Jews struggled to keep their balance as the trucks bumped their way toward the forest, repeatedly knocking one another over like a nightmarish game of human dominos. No one knew where they were going, but everyone understood that it was nowhere good.

After driving for a few kilometers, the trucks reached an area of forest near the village of Stanevitsh. At gunpoint, several of the Jews were told to dig a large pit. They began shoveling, their bodies shaking and eyes welling as the hopeless reality of what they were doing crystallized. Many cried out in anguish.

Once the men finished shoveling, the Nazis selected roughly twenty-five Jews, lined them up along the edge of the open pit, and opened fire. Over the course of six hours, the Nazis and their collaborators did the same with another group of Jews, and another, and another, until all of the transported men were left discarded in the graves that they had dug for themselves.

Two hundred and twenty *intelligentsia*, or influential citizens, from Iwje were murdered that day as the sound of gunfire echoed through the town. Most survivors understood the fate that befell their family, leaders, and friends; widows became suicidal upon hearing the news. Others still clung to the false hope offered by the Gestapo that their loved ones were alive and well, transported to work camps in the west.

5

Home to about 5,000 people, Serniki was surrounded by forest and marshes.[1] The primary source of livelihood was farming for the mostly impoverished population, with some Jews working as artisans or tradesmen. About 1,000 Sernikians were Jewish, though the numbers felt greater to those who lived within the tight-knit Jewish neighborhoods that dated back centuries.[2] Serniki was largely populated by Ukrainians, though some Polish nationals had also moved in after the Great War left the area under Polish control.[3] Depending on their origins, the residents spoke Yiddish, Polish, or Ukrainian. They lived in harmony, typically keeping to their own, but intermingling in schools and stores without incident.

In September 1938, after attending a series of *cheydas*, Paula Silberfarb began public school. At seven years old, Paula was years younger than the non-Jewish students who started first grade at later ages, and so she generally stuck with her Jewish peers. Paula loved school. She excelled in math and language and effortlessly fell into the teacher's favor with her sweet and cooperative demeanor.

When a new student, Rodel, arrived in class, Paula quickly befriended her. Rodel's father made a good living as a pharmacist and, in contrast to the small wood homes that crowded the streets of Serniki, he moved his family into a large house on a hilltop. A brick staircase surrounded by colorful roses led up to the grand residence, equipped with Roman columns and dark stained-glass windows. The girls quickly became inseparable.

All summer long, Paula eagerly awaited the first day of second grade. She was excited to no longer be among the youngest in the school and to learn more complex arithmetic. But in September 1939, just as the school year was set to begin, the Soviets invaded Serniki.

Under Soviet rule, the stores in Serniki were shuttered. Samuel, no longer able to continue with his boatmaking business, struggled to provide for his family. The Silberfarbs relied heavily on the food grown in their garden and care packages sent from Samuel's sister Bebble in Kiev containing money and clothing for the children. Bebble wrote frequent letters with stern reminders that Samuel must not operate his business or otherwise disobey Soviet orders, emphasizing that the consequences would be shipment to Siberia. Lea and Samuel bore much of the stress quietly, attempting to minimize the disruption to their children's lives.

Despite being a top student, Paula was forced to repeat the entire first-grade curriculum. She was required to learn Russian before advancing. Frustrated but undeterred, Paula spent evenings studying the Russian alphabet. Samuel was fluent in the language from his time in Kiev and sat at the bedroom table with Paula for hours, teaching her to read and write. By the end of the year, Paula was approved for second grade.

Serniki was relatively isolated, and only the occasional rumor about the happenings in Nazi Germany reached the village. Nobody had heard about the *aktionen*, or mass exterminations, until early summer of 1941. On a quiet, sunny day, a father and son suddenly came rushing out of the forest that abutted the town. They were naked, caked in dirt and grime, and panting so heavily that their screaming bordered on incoherent. The men frantically tried to grab the attention of whomever they could find, as passersby sought to dodge the seemingly insane men shouting in the street. Lea listened.

The men recounted that they had come from a nearby *shtetl* that the Germans had recently invaded. All of the Jews in their town had been ordered to report to the local market for registration, at which time they were marched to the edge of a ditch. The Gestapo forced the Jews at gunpoint to line up and undress. They then opened fire on the Jews, shooting their naked bodies into a mass grave. The man and his son fell into the ditch before the bullets hit them and feigned death amid the pile of warm twitching corpses. At night, after the guards had left, they climbed out from the pit and ran into the forest.

With a single exception, none of the Jews in Serniki believed the men's tale, which quickly spread through the community. The Serniki Jews rationalized that the father and son must be infirm or beggars seeking to play on locals' sympathy. Crediting the tale meant upending their lives and facing the reality of the holocaust developing around them. Some Jews even hoped for a German invasion, thinking that they would at least be permitted to reopen their businesses.

Paula asked her mother whether the story was true. Lea looked at her, eyes dark with fear. "Nobody can make up a story like that," Lea said. "It has to be true."

Lea took the traumatized father and son into her home. She fed them, clothed them, and offered them a place to spend the night.

Just weeks after the two Jews had arrived, the Red Army began packing. In late June, it retreated. The fleeing Soviets offered to take along any residents wanting to leave, but most declined. There was still no visible sign of a German encroachment, and the Ukrainian and Polish residents felt no loyalty to the communists.[4]

By early July 1941, Serniki fell within German territory. Outwardly, however, it remained unoccupied. The small town had little strategic value to the Germans, who viewed establishing a physical presence there as a low priority.[5]

The absence of communist or fascist rule created a power vacuum in Serniki. Local Ukrainians, mainly young men emboldened with guns, anointed themselves as a police force. These rogue citizens terrorized the Jews of Serniki, ransacking houses and assaulting and raping their Jewish neighbors.[6] Many Jews began hiding their valuables, stashing bedding and jewelry in attics and under floorboards. Lea and Samuel brought their few expensive belongings to Samuel's friend, a non-Jewish farmer who lived on the outskirts of Serniki, for safekeeping.

But as pogroms broke out and attacks and murders of Jews grew increasingly normalized, the Silberfarbs decided that they had to flee. Lea and Samuel took their three children to the farmer's house. The decision upended their lives, but outside the population center and hidden among non-Jews, they were at least safe from the mobs.

A few days after they had left, Samuel's father, Gershon, stopped by the Silberfarb house to check that it had not been damaged in the looting. Finding the house unscathed and vacant, Gershon walked around back to the vegetable garden hoping to find a potato or two that could be dug out and eaten for dinner. As Gershon stood in the garden inspecting the plants, Daniello Polohovitch, a Ukrainian local, walked onto the property and shot Gershon dead in broad daylight.

Daniello skipped off toward the marketplace, busting into Fannie's house. "I shot old Gershon! I shot old Gershon in the garden!" he taunted Gershon's sister. Fannie was stunned, both by the news and the man who now stood inside her home proclaiming his guilt with glee. After confirming that the story was true—Gershon's body was found abandoned in the Silberfarbs' garden—Fannie sent word to Samuel and his family to come home. Fannie also made arrangements for the body to be moved to her home so the family could pay their respects before burial.

Hearing the news, the Silberfarbs returned to Serniki. They found their home and the adjacent apartment vacant. The Neiditzes had fled, somehow managing to arrange transport to stay with family in Canada. Samuel spent the night at Fannie's house, wanting to be with his father's body; according to the Jewish tradition of *Shemira*, a deceased body must be watched over until burial. Lea stayed with the children. Reasoning that the small apartment was a less-appealing target than their attached home, Lea decided that she and the children would sleep in the studio.

That night, Lea was awakened by a loud banging coming from her house next door. Realizing that locals were looting the home, Lea stirred the children and hurried them under a bed. "Shhh," she said, trying to remain calm. "Pretend you're little mice." The children and their mother scurried under a single bed, their heads barely peeking out the edge.

The Silberfarbs held their breath as they carefully monitored the sound of footsteps, struggling to discern if they were growing closer or farther away. They could hear the bangs of drawers being ripped open and cabinets slammed shut, their most personal possessions being ransacked. The children quietly prayed that the men did not also try to break into the apartment.

Eventually the interlopers disappeared into the night. When Lea checked on the house in the morning, she found it pillaged; floorboards had been pried off, furniture broken, and anything remotely valuable had disappeared.

Gershon was quickly buried. After the funeral, the Silberfarbs stopped by his house. Gershon's daughter, Pola, had already moved out, relocating with her husband and baby to a smaller apartment farther from the town center. The once-lively home, filed with laughter and prayers, was eerily silent.

Samuel spent the subsequent days at Fannie's house, sitting *shiva*. In Judaism, the nuclear family of a deceased relative spends the seven days following burial together in mourning. As part of the ritual, the *Mourner's Kaddish* is recited daily during prayer, requiring the presence of a ten-person *minyan*, or quorum.

One quiet Wednesday in August, after her husband left for the *minyan*, Lea sent Paula and Sophia to fetch a pail of water from the river. The girls were carrying the bucket back to the house when they saw Lea running toward them frantically. "Hurry, *schnel, schnel!*" she yelled as soon as she was within earshot of the girls. "The Germans are here!" Paula paused, confused. The town had seemed peaceful to her and Sophia on their walk.

Lea grabbed the bucket from the girls' hands and dragged them into the nearest yard. As Lea pulled them down behind the home's front bushes, Paula still could not understand why her mother was suddenly so panicked. "Where are the Germans?" Paula asked.

"Shhh, right here!" Lea whispered.

Paula lifted her gaze to see two horses towering over her. Atop of each horse sat a soldier, wearing an unfamiliar uniform: a helmet with a matching greenish-grey suit, tall leather boots, and a long gun strapped behind his left shoulder. From the ten-year-old's perspective, the men looked like Goliath, both in size and might. She nervously crouched down lower.

Once the horses had passed and continued down the street, Lea and the girls hurried to the apartment. As they were running, Daniello and other self-appointed local police gave chase. "Every Jew to the market!" they shouted.

Lea calmly turned to the Ukrainian men behind her, her children in tow. "I am just going to drop off the pail of water at my house, and we will go," she said matter-of-factly.

"Okay, put the water down and then go, fast" one of the men shouted back.

Lea and the girls sprinted into the house to find Bernie waiting. Outside they could hear the shouts of men herding Jews into the town center. German soldiers were walking door-to-door, snatching Jews from their homes at gunpoint. Lea and the children did not have much time. "We are not going to the market," Lea announced. "We are running away, or they are going to kill us."

Paula, haunted by the two men's story of mass killing in their village and trusting her mother, immediately agreed. Sophia comprehended less of the situation but cooperated, sensing the terror in the room. Bernie refused. "We have to go because Daddy is in Fannie's house!" he said defiantly.

"Either they caught him or he escaped," Lea explained to her twelve-year-old son, shuffling him to the back of the house. "But I cannot take you to the market or they will kill you."

Lea persuaded Bernie that they should run away to the farmer's house where they had hidden earlier that summer. After checking the windows to confirm that nobody was surveilling the house and reminding her children to move quickly and quietly, Lea opened the back door. The four Silberfarbs snuck outside and disappeared into the wheat field behind the vegetable garden. They ran through a series of fields, crossing streets only when necessary and only in non-Jewish areas with no police presence. When Lea and the children were about halfway to the farmer's house, Bernie suddenly stopped running.

"I'm not leaving without Daddy," Bernie insisted. Before Lea had an opportunity to reason with him, Bernie turned around and took off back toward Serniki. Lea assumed that all the Jews who went to the market in Serniki would be killed. Determined to keep Paula and Sophia alive, she put on a brave face, squeezed the girls' hands tightly, and continued running in the opposite direction of her son. Lea's head was haunted by thoughts of the Nazis opening fire on her husband and son.

As Lea and the girls approached the farmer's house, they found him working outside. He greeted them warmly. Though tears, Lea explained what had happened in their Jewish neighborhood and that she feared her husband and son may be in the marketplace.

"Don't worry," the farmer said. "I will go and investigate. You stay here." The farmer hid Lea and the girls in a pile of hay in his barn, keeping them covered in case any police were to search the property. He then headed off toward the town center.

The three Silberfarbs stayed put for hours, lying still underneath the hot and itchy hay, their noses eventually growing numb to the putrid scent of cow manure. Lea sang softly to her frightened girls, trying to keep them—and herself—calm. As nightfall set in, the farmer returned.

"They took everybody to the market," he explained. "But the women and children were sent back home." He said that the Germans cut off the Jewish men's beards and forced them to work, assigning tasks like washing horses and soldiers' socks. "I didn't see your husband there, but they killed one boy. I don't know who."

Lea's stomach sank. In her gut she felt that the young boy must have been Bernie, punished for attempting to flee.

Given that the Germans were not detaining women and children, the farmer encouraged Lea to take Paula and Sophia and head home. "You don't have to worry," he said. Lea did not want to return to Serniki. She knew that it was only a matter of time before the Germans escalated their violence. But feeling uncomfortable overstaying her welcome, Lea thanked the farmer for his kindness and left.

As they were walking, Lea determined that it would be safer to stay on the edge of town where they could more quickly escape to the woods if necessary. Samuel had a cousin, Shlenke, who lived near the Stubla River. Lea decided to approach Shlenke's house to see whether it was inhabited. If people were home, it would be safe to spend the night with the girls. If the lights were off, Lea would know something was wrong. In that case, she planned to hide under the rickety wooden bridge that traversed the river until she could figure out where to take the girls in the morning.

The lights were on in Shlenke's house. As Lea and the girls walked in, they were stunned to find Bernie sitting at the table. Lea pulled her son against her chest, hugging him tightly. "What happened to you?" she asked.

Bernie explained that he had gone to the market looking for Samuel. "Daddy wasn't there, but the Germans caught me. They asked me my age. I told them I was twelve and they sent me home, saying I was too young to work." Not knowing where else to go, Bernie ran to Shlenke's house.

The next morning, a Thursday, Lea left the children with Shlenke and took a walk to the market, hoping to figure out where Samuel had gone. She saw hundreds of Jews working for the Germans. She recognized many browbeaten faces in the crowd, friends and extended family members, but there was no sign of Samuel. Hoping he was hidden away somewhere safe, Lea returned to Shlenke's home.

On Friday morning, Lea and her children heard the pops of rapid gunfire in the distance. Lea ran out from the house to investigate what was happening. As she neared the marketplace, a non-Jewish man approached her. "They killed all the people at the cemetery." He explained that the Germans had a pit dug out near the village cemetery where they shot the Jewish men. "Your husband said to tell your son that he should say *Kaddish* for him."

Lea, in disbelief, questioned the man. "But my husband, he wasn't there yesterday?"

The man shook his head. "Your husband was there."

6

Within a few weeks, the Nazis cordoned off a several-block radius as a Jewish Quarter in Iwje. Jews residing outside the designated area were removed from their homes and forced into the houses of other Jews already living inside the Quarter. The Bakszts were ordered to immediately evacuate their residence and permitted to take only what little they could carry in their bare hands. Like many others, they were forced to live in an overcrowded house with multiple families.

In the new quarters, David and his siblings slept in a small living room, which functioned as a bedroom for all the children in the house as well as a dining area. The other equally crowded bedrooms were used to accommodate the remaining twenty or so adults. The Germans and local police, meanwhile, seized the newly vacant dwellings for themselves.

The Germans began promulgating anti-Jewish decrees, adding new restrictions on what seemed like a daily basis. Jews were prohibited from eating dietary staples like meat, butter, and eggs.[1] No alcohol could be consumed, including the wine needed for religious services.[2] It became a crime for the Iwje Jews to contact any non-Jew or even other Jews residing outside of the town.[3]

To facilitate communications with the Jewish Quarter, the Nazis forced the Jews to select a *Judenrat*. The *Judenrat* was a council of Jews that served as internal enforcers and liaisons for the Germans. When local officers and more senior officials from Lida demanded money and specific goods—gold watches, furniture, men's suits—it fell to the *Judenrat* to carry out their wishes.[4] Multiple times per week, members of the *Judenrat* ran frantically around the Jewish Quarter collecting the requested items, knowing that if they did not return within thirty minutes, Jews would be shot.[5] As time went on, the requests became more unreasonable given the few possessions that the Iwje Jews still had, though each one was somehow ultimately fulfilled.[6]

The Jews who remained alive continued to spend their days struggling through manual labor and avoiding the wrath of their supervisors. The *Judenrat* had set up workshops where Jews produced goods for the Germans, believing the promises that hard work would keep them alive.[7] But anyone who appeared ill was immediately shot by the police, and without proper hygiene and medical care, typhus, lice, and skin diseases were rampant. The Nazis supplied meager amounts of food, leaving many to die of malnutrition. Others who made it to winter froze to death without heat or proper clothing.

David was put to work in a small ladder factory with seventeen other men. One day they heard a knock on the door. A voice said in Yiddish, "Let me in." When they opened the door, they met a man standing with a long rifle across his shoulders. "I've come to take you to the forest," he announced. "Follow me."

The men had heard rumors of Jews escaping to the woods, and many, including David, wished to go with the rescuer. But others protested, afraid that the Nazis would retaliate. "Please don't go," they cried, "the Nazis will notice you've escaped and kill our families." Not wanting to jeopardize the safety of their friends and families, the factory workers agreed to stay in Iwje. The rescuer left with a heavy heart.

In late 1941, Berko devised a plan. He had heard stories of skilled Jews who were permitted to ply their trade instead of being relegated to hard labor and wanted to rescue his sons from the daily oppression. Winter was fast approaching, and Berko understood how valuable leather was to German soldiers who used it to make coats, pants, and boots. He knew the basics of leathermaking from watching his father and that a small leathermaking factory now sat abandoned on the outskirts of Iwje after the Nazis forced its Jewish owner into labor.

Relying on his pre-occupation business connections, Berko snuck away to a non-Jewish Pole and presented the idea of leathermaking. The Polish man thought that it was a promising proposal and agreed to serve as an intermediary with the Germans. He approached a few Nazi soldiers and relayed that he knew a Jew who could produce leather for them. The Nazis were eager at the prospect of a local leather source and asked to speak with Berko directly. Berko, communicating with the officers in German, explained the basics of leathermaking. He said that he could produce it for them in the old factory as long as he be permitted to move about Iwje freely to obtain supplies and given the assistance of the prior owner and some additional workers. The Nazis, impressed with Berko's language skills, took the bait.

Berko brought the extended Bakszt family and the prior owner and his family to work in the factory. The job offered a welcomed respite from the watchful eyes of the Germans and their accomplices, though leather tanning was not an easy task. The workers softened and washed the skins in water, rubbing off leftover blood and fat with their bare fingers. They then soaked the hide in salt or another alkaline solution, which helped loosen hair follicles and ease the next step of scraping off the hair. After a series of soaking and resting, the hide was hand beaten, kneaded, and stretched before being submerged for weeks in tannic acids derived from pine tree bark. The tannins colored the leather and made it more resistant to water, bacteria, and breakage. Once the months-long process was complete, the leather was polished with whatever grease could be found—milk, animal fats, or oils—and ready for delivery to the Germans.

The leathermaking factory kept the Bakszts relatively safe and fed. Berko now had a reason to frequent with the town's secular population, from whom he acquired supplies and animal skins (which they were required by ordinance to preserve from slaughtered cattle) as well as updates on the war. He heard about Germany's expansion across Europe and the Soviet Union, and the Americans' recently formalized involvement. The Nazis in Iwje were satisfied with their new leather supply and in exchange did not pry into the Bakszts' activities. To the Germans' ignorance, Berko was secretly stockpiling some of the leather, which he traded with local farmers to feed his own family and workers.

By early May 1942, tension was building in Iwje. A total of 1,000 Jews from nearby villages had been transported into the town in several batches, and each time the Iwje Jews were forced to absorb them into the unbearably overcrowded Jewish Quarter.[8] The *Judenrat* divided up the new arrivals and assigned them to homes.[9] Gestapo officers were also increasing in numbers and demands. They buckled down on workers and ordered all Jews to shave their heads. News quickly spread of several new *aktionen* happening in nearby towns, including as close by as in Lida.

On May 8, 1942, rows of German police appeared in the Iwje marketplace, engaged in military exercises with their weapons. The proffered reasons for their presence varied. Some Jews heard that the soldiers were being sent to the front to combat the Soviets; others relayed that the officials were preparing to raid the nearby forest to target guerrilla fighters.[10] The most obvious explanation was that Iwje was next on the long list of mass exterminations happening in the region.

Over the following days, the Jewish Quarter swarmed with police. Most of the Jews were ordered to stay inside their homes, prohibited from even using the outhouses. They spent the days peering out windows, hungry and anxious about what might happen next. Limited exemptions were given for urgent business, allowing the Bakszts and their associates to continue working in the factory. In the evenings, they returned to a dejected community.

On May 11, the Germans sent word via the *Judenrat* that if the Jews collected enough gold rubles, the town would be spared from any violence. The Jews, overjoyed, volunteered what meager amounts they could until the money was assembled.[11] That night, as many Iwje Jews fell into a proper sleep for the first time in days, the Nazis quietly seized dozens of physically fit men. The Jewish men were led from the Quarter into the Stanevitsh Forest and ordered to dig large pits.

The early morning hours of May 12, 1942, in Iwje were outwardly peaceful. The sun shined down warmly on the rural fields surrounding the town, and the scent of morning dew and blooming florals filled the air.[12] Then the men returned, catapulting the Jewish Quarter into hysterics as they explained that they spent the night digging graves. But there was no means of escape; the Jewish Quarter was surrounded by Gestapo officers and dogs before dawn.

Suddenly the silent streets teemed with the sounds of thunderous engines and shouting. The Germans and their collaborators—Polish police and Lithuanian troops drunk on power and whisky[13]—scoured the Jewish Quarter, searching homes and ordering the Jews into the market. The Nazis and their collaborators warned that anyone caught hiding would be shot in place; they executed a baby, left in its crib by desperate parents.[14] The Jews, many not yet even dressed, were chased from their homes by whip-wielding police.[15] Children and elderly Jews who ran too slowly were beaten or killed, turning the streets red with blood.[16] The Lithuanians tormented the Jews, gesturing as though they would slit the Jews' necks and laughing wickedly as they marched distraught families to the marketplace.[17]

With nowhere to hide in the Quarter, the Bakszts had no choice but to proceed to the market square. When they arrived, they found thousands of Jews standing with their families, surrounded by police with guns and whips. The Bakszts quickly merged into the faceless crowd. Jews were grouped by family and directed onwards to a nearby intersection, where several Gestapo officers were waiting. After scrutinizing the Jews standing before them for a few moments, the officers ordered the Jews to proceed in one of three directions: right to Moshchizki Street, left to Gimenna Street, or straight toward a Catholic church.[18]

Berko and Rochel waited with their family until a German soldier accompanied by a local Pole called them forward. The Pole recognized Berko as the manager of the leather factory, and the entire family was directed to the left. The Bakszts continued walking, their feet propelling them forward almost mindlessly as their heads frantically searched around trying to determine where they were being sent. As they proceeded, the Bakszts could see that those in front of them and those sent to the right were being lined up and held in place. Many were people they recognized, families headed by local doctors and physically fit men. Those ordered forward, seemingly large families with several young children or the elderly, were marching onward in the direction of Stanevitsh.

After walking a few meters, the Bakszts heard another soldier shouting, "Get down with your heads on the ground. If you lift your head, you'll be shot."

As they bent over, David could hear Berko sternly instruct everyone, "Lie down and don't do anything."

The Bakszt family, from the youngest Gussie to the eldest Chana, pressed their heads into the dirt.

They were technically permitted to speak, but it was impossible to hear anything over the drum of distant gunfire. Some Jews who had money or jewelry on their persons buried the valuables in the ground underneath their bodies, hoping they could retrieve the items later or at least avoid turning them over to the Nazis. Others simply prayed. Every few minutes a piercing scream or violent grunt would briefly distract from the steady rat-tat-tat of machine guns.

The Bakszts lay in the hot street for hours, listening to the sounds of their friends and extended family being murdered, unable to see anything but the ground beneath them. As evening set in, a German official ordered the remaining Jews to stand up and turn in their valuables. S.S. Officer Rudolf Werner stood with an open sack, collecting money, gold, and jewelry from the Jews.[19] A commander who oversaw the selection, Leopold Windisch, then appeared in the marketplace and delivered a short speech in German to the surviving Jews:

> *The Jews are at fault for both world wars. They incited the Allies to annihilate Germany; therefore it is only logical that the German government should exterminate all the Jews to blame for the catastrophe. You are only remaining alive provisionally—depending on the status at the front; at the first major setback on the front, you will all be murdered.*[20]

The Jews were told that, in the meantime, they were expected to pay for their lives by working for the Reich.[21]

That day, the Nazis and their associates killed approximately 2,500 men, women, and children in Iwje. The Jews were paraded to the trenches in Stanevitsh, cognizant of the fate that awaited them. The police closely monitored the Jews as they marched the three-kilometer distance. Weak grandparents and tired children were shot in place and without warning, falling at the feet of their horrified families who were forced to keep moving or else meet the same fate. Desperate men attempted to attack the guards, barely managing to inflict any injuries before being pummeled by a spray of bullets. One woman, struggling to soothe her crying child as he lay cradled in her arms, was approached by a soldier who smacked the child in the head with a hand grenade.[22] The baby, killed instantly, tumbled from his screaming mother's arms onto the dirt ground.[23] Most Jews prayed quietly and wept, resigned to the impossible situation. It was rumored that Alter Gershovitz—either refusing to go to his grave in solemnity or "mad from terror"—walked the entire distance singing songs with his wife.[24]

When they arrived at the pits, the Jews were ordered forward in groups of one to two dozen at a time and forced to undress and set aside their clothing and any valuables in a growing pile. The naked adults were lined up and shot into the pit. Not wanting to waste their bullets on children, the Nazis and their collaborators threw babies and youngsters into the ditch alive, leaving them to suffocate under the crushing weight of the bodies piling on top of them.[25] A similar death befell those not instantly killed by the ammunition, who spent their last moments gasping for breath. All the while, the dwindling remaining Jews looked on. The Nazis repeated the process until all 2,500 Jews had been murdered, pausing only to ingest their schnapps and sausages.[26]

The 1,000 Iwje Jews spared from selection were herded into a ghetto comprising just a few small streets. Jews frantically ran into homes, desperate to once again secure a place for their families to take shelter. After the masses retreated into houses, the Polish police rounded up fifty young men to cover the pits in Stanevitsh.[27] The men were forced to drag anyone lying on the surrounding ground into the pits and to cover the naked bodies with calcium oxide and dirt.[28] Every so often, a man would let out a stifled wail, recognizing a friend or family member in the pile of abandoned bodies. German and Polish authorities looked on, guarding the Jews and shooting at any bodies that exhibited signs of life.[29] Leopold Windisch stood shouting, "Quick, quick, away with the Jewish shit!"[30]

7

The Iwje ghetto was wretched. It was surrounded by fencing topped with barbed wire and monitored by police from the outside. Inside, it was filled with beggars. People lived in unbearably cramped conditions. The Bakszts moved into a house where their uncle was already living. The three-room residence now held four families, totaling seventeen people. Basic supplies and services were lacking. Garbage was left piled in streets, reeking in the hot sun, and plumbing backed up without repair. Unsanitary conditions meant that diseases spread rampantly. Like countless others, Alter Gershovitz's youngest son, Yitzhak, died of typhus.[1]

The Nazis worked the Jews to their breaking point, providing mere scraps of food for sustenance. Some Jews were able to smuggle in food from outside sources or send small children to crawl out through gaps in the ghetto wall. Jewish "police" ordered to patrol the fences looked the other way when captives chose to bend the wires and sneak out to trade their measly possessions for food from peasants.[2] Those without an alternative food source starved.

Every day was spent laboring to the point of exhaustion, fighting to just survive to the next day. Small factories were set up inside the ghetto, where Jews produced goods for the Germans like shoe polish, candles, baskets, and rope.[3] Some were tasked with carpentry work, such as building coffins for German soldiers killed by Soviet guerrilla fighters.[4] Others demolished homes, unloaded German trucks, chopped wood in the forest, and laid train tracks.

Berko continued to manufacture leather. He and his workforce were issued special documents permitting them to leave the ghetto early each morning and return each evening. Berko's workers gained a reputation as the "chosen ones" among ghetto Jews; they were subject to limited oversight during the day and privy to a backdoor food supply thanks to Berko's dealings.

Amid the misery, the ghetto prisoners attempted to maintain some semblance of normalcy. Each morning and evening, a short religious service was held so people could recite the *Mourner's Kaddish*. Jews occasionally socialized, and life milestones, the Sabbath, and religious holidays were acknowledged to the extent feasible. When one of David's aunts got married, the family held a small ceremony in the house, wished the couple *mazel tov*, and shared a piece of bread.

Outside the barbed wires, the resistance movement was growing. Thousands of Soviet soldiers left behind after the German invasion took to the woods.[5] They were joined by Soviet prisoners of war who had escaped German custody after being released on work duty and local Polish men who objected to Nazi violence.[6] These partisans survived by raiding German outposts and forcing locals to feed and temporarily shelter them. As partisan numbers grew, the Soviet Union sent men to organize, weaponize, and train the fighters, though they continued to function as predominately discrete units.[7]

At the same time, more Jews began seeking refuge in the forests, escaping from ghettos and Nazi *aktionen*. These fugitives, often families with young children or elderly parents, were not typically welcome guests. In addition to harboring antisemitic views, the Soviet partisans viewed the Jews as liabilities with few skills or weapons to contribute to the opposition movement.[8] Often, Soviet partisans robbed and assaulted the Jewish escapees they encountered in the forest.[9]

One exception to this was the Bielski Otriad. Established in the summer of 1942,[10] it was led by three brothers—Tuvia, Asael, and Zus Bielski—who had grown up in a large Jewish family in Stanevitsh.[11] The Bielski brothers' parents and two of their siblings had been killed by the Germans in the Nowogrodek ghetto[12] in an *aktion* that killed 4,000 Jews,[13] including David's girlfriend, Macha, and her parents.[14] The brothers escaped to the woods.[15] Unlike many of the Soviet fighter groups, under Tuvia Bielski's command, the Bielski Partisans prioritized saving Jews over seeking vengeance against the Nazis.[16] Joined by extended family and friends, the group undertook significant efforts to liberate Jews from nearby ghettos and welcomed women, children, and the elderly into its ranks.[17] It grew from an initial group of thirty to ultimately include more than 1,200 people.[18]

News of these partisan groups permeated the Iwje ghetto. Jews who traveled outside the barbed-wire walls as part of their work detail encountered Soviet partisans near the forest edge. Ghetto inmates began to organize, amassing weaponry and establishing contact with partisan units to whom they could eventually flee.[19] They built underground hideaways in ghetto homes and kept watch in attics for indications of an imminent *aktion*.[20] Ellie Bakszt was active in these preparations; he smuggled rifle parts and ammunition into the ghetto and readied his friends for an armed defensive.[21]

Berko also began to connect with partisans while running the leather factory. Friendly farmers served as intermediaries, delivering updates on movements in the region. Berko continued to hear stories of ghetto liquidations and concentration camps with gas chambers. He knew that their time in Iwje was limited. Seeking to protect his family and fellow Jews, Berko worked with these trusted farmers to link escaping ghetto Jews with partisans in the surrounding forests. The process required that the Jews travel dozens of kilometers on foot without detection. It necessitated meticulous planning, with meeting spots, rest stops, and meals all prearranged.

Berko's primary role in these escape plots was to get the Jews out of the Iwje ghetto without raising suspicions. If their plans were discovered, Berko risked not just the lives of the runaways but also those of everyone involved in the operation, including his family and the factory workers. Berko began bribing the ghetto guards with extra leather to look the other way as his morning work detail exceeded his eighteen-person allotment. The additional Jews walked with Berko and his regular workforce from the ghetto to the leather factory. They were then directed to predetermined meeting places, where they were hidden during daylight hours and sent to the woods at night. At the end of the workday, Berko returned to the ghetto with his eighteen Jewish workers and more leather to appease any inquisitive guards.

Over the course of several months, Berko successfully smuggled dozens of Jews out of the Iwje ghetto to various partisan groups. This included a large chunk of Rochel's extended family, the original owner of the leather factory and his relatives, and numerous other Jews who saw the forest as an attractive alternative to ghetto life.

Berko also did what he could to help his extended family in more remote locations. His wife had distant relatives, the Baran family, living about 200 kilometers south of Iwje in the Krasne ghetto. Though Berko had never himself met the Barans, he paid a non-Jewish man to locate them and deliver food, reasoning that the family of six would likely be starving under the circumstances.

As winter set in, Ellie, barely eighteen, decided to sneak out and join the Bielski Brigade. Berko eventually heard that Ellie had made it into the forest and located the group safely, but details of his whereabouts were sparse. When rumors of an impending liquidation reached the Iwje ghetto two weeks later, Berko decided that it was time for the rest of his family to seek refuge as well.

One morning, just days before New Year's Eve, Berko took Rochel, David, Batya, and Gussie, as well as Rochel's sister and her immediate family, to the factory. They planned to join up with the Bielski Partisans, knowing of Tuvia's policy of welcoming full families and hoping to reunite with Ellie. Berko and Rochel begged Rochel's mother, Chana, to join them, insisting that staying in the ghetto was too dangerous. Chana refused. "*Kinderlach*," she said, "you go and save yourselves. Don't worry about me." With no choice but to leave her behind, Berko and Rochel said their painful goodbyes, knowing that they were unlikely to see Chana again.

Instead of returning to the ghetto that evening, the Bakszts went into the attic of the factory and hid until dark. Under the cover of night, Berko led everyone behind the factory and into the woods. It was a frigid night, but Berko insisted that they remain a couple of hundred feet inside the snowy forest, out of sight of the road but close enough to maintain their orientation. Gussie, ten years old, struggled to walk in the two to three feet of snow that layered the ground and reached as high as her waist. Berko picked up the young girl and placed her on his shoulders. The family trekked onward.

A few hours later, David sensed that the weight of Gussie coupled with Berko's hernia was taking its toll on Berko. David's father lagged behind, his pace progressively slowing as he trudged through the thick snow. "Dad, you must be very tired," David said, turning around. "Let me take her." Berko immediately acquiesced. Knowing that his father was not one to accept help, David felt his stomach sink. Berko must have been struggling far more than he had let on.

After walking through the night, the Bakszt family reached the Bielski Partisans and reunited with Ellie. The young man was in and out of the campsite, frequently sent off on sabotage missions to blow up bridges and train tracks used by the Nazis to reach the front.

The group was welcoming, but the conditions were unbearable. The Otriad had only recently relocated to the Chrapiniewo Forest near Iwje after a warning of an imminent German attack had forced them to abandon their more established campsites in the Perelaz and Zabiełowo Forests.[22] The frozen ground made digging holes challenging, so only a handful of primitive tents had been constructed.[23] The Bakszts were forced to sleep on the snow. Food was also scarce, as the partisans struggled to establish a reliable food supply in their new location. The

Bakszt children tried not to complain, but by the next day their feet were literally freezing.

While the Bakszts were with the Bielski Otriad, Tuvia Bielski sent four armed men to the Iwje ghetto to warn the prisoners of the impending liquidation.[24] Given the advance notice, when the Nazis arrived en masse on New Year's Eve, Jewish watchmen in ghetto attics immediately spotted their approach. More than one hundred Jews were able to cut the wire fencing at the other end of the ghetto and escape to the woods.[25] Throughout the night Jews continued to sneak out of the ghetto, emerging in drips and drabs between rounds of German and Polish police patrols.[26]

The runaway Iwjeans made it to the Zabiełowo Forest, where they were received by Tuvia and a twenty-person training crew.[27] Over several days, the Iwje Jews learned how to survive in the woods.[28] Tuvia and his men divided the Iwje Jews into subgroups, helped them elect leaders, and taught them how to forage for food and defend themselves.[29]

By early January, concerns about an attack on the Bielskis had subsided, and some partisans began to return to their prior campsites.[30] On January 5, 1943, a small group of partisans, including the Bielski brothers' wives and extended families, asked Tuvia's permission to spend the night in a couple of farm homes near the village of Chrapiniewo.[31] Tuvia was uneasy with the idea of having several partisans in the local community; it was just days after the Iwje ghetto rescue, and the Nazis had a 50,000 Reichsmark bounty out on Tuvia's head.[32] But pitying his sister-in-law who was ill with the flu, Tuvia gave his reluctant consent.[33] He sent along a few fighters for the women's security,[34] including Ellie.

The group approached two homes.[35] The owners, aware that the partisans were armed, agreed to allow the Jews to spend the night.[36] In one of the two houses, Chaja Bielski (Asael's wife) prepared food for her sisters-in-law, Ellie, and a few other guards, as the men cleaned their guns.[37] While the partisans relaxed, relieved to be out of the cold, Chaja remained on edge.[38] She was concerned that the Germans might have somehow followed the Iwje ghetto escapees to their area.[39] Though there was a partisan guard sitting watch on the main road,⁴⁰ Chaja repeatedly stepped outside to monitor the homes' perimeters.⁴¹ But the biting cold and whiteout conditions quickly forced her back inside each time.⁴²

During one such attempt, Chaja noticed the vague figures of men camouflaged in long white coats nearing the homes.⁴³ She burst inside screaming, "We are surrounded!"⁴⁴ The Germans and local police killed the partisan guard and quickly encircled the two farmhouses with hundreds of men.⁴⁵

Initially they held their fire, hoping to capture some of the partisans alive and gather intelligence about Tuvia's movements.⁴⁶ "Hurrah Bielski, Hurrah Bielski," they jeered.⁴⁷ But the Bielski Partisans began shooting, and the Germans attacked the houses.⁴⁸ Ellie and the other partisan guards continued firing at the Nazis—helping provide the cover for Zus and Asael's wives to escape—until they ran out of bullets.⁴⁹

Tuvia, who was training the Iwje Jews, learned of the attack.⁵⁰ He rushed to the homes, finding them engulfed in fire with dead bodies strewn about.⁵¹ Nine of the twelve Jews, including Tuvia's wife, were killed by the Nazis.⁵² Ellie was found shot dead as he attempted to escape, his body collapsed on a fence separating the property from the nearby forest.

One partisan, Lova Volkin, was captured alive by the Germans and brutally tortured; they ripped out his nails, cut off his fingers, and gouged out his eyes, but he never gave away the location of the Bielskis' camp.⁵³ Volkin was eventually hanged in the center of Nowogrodek with a sign stating, "This is what will happen to every Jew who leaves the ghetto."⁵⁴ The deaths were the first casualties suffered by the Bielski unit since its establishment.⁵⁵

The partisans broke the news of Ellie's death to the Bakszt family, though many of the details were omitted.⁵⁶ Unbeknownst to the Bakszts, Ellie's body was not left abandoned on the fence. The local police commander recruited a group of men to bury the deceased partisans.⁵⁷ With fifteen Belorussian locals looking on, the partisans were covered in an unmarked pit that night.⁵⁸

Shortly thereafter, a distraught Berko and Rochel realized that they could not continue living in the woods with the Bielskis. Even if no further German attacks materialized, the brutal winter created insufferable hazards. They grew increasingly concerned that their children, especially Gussie, would develop severe hypothermia or frostbite. Picking what they thought to be the lesser of two evils, they made the difficult decision to return to Iwje.

8

Shortly after the shooting, Lea Silberfarb's brother, Avraham, found her at Schlenke's house. Lea was quiet, focused on devising a plan to save her children as a newly single parent. The situation forced Lea to compartmentalize, depriving her of the opportunity to properly mourn her husband's murder.

Avraham confirmed that Samuel had been killed in the *aktion*. He said that after saying *Kaddish* on Wednesday morning, Samuel had gone into the small, empty store attached to Fannie's house looking for a quiet place to take a nap. When Samuel awoke, he could hear the screaming. Out the window he saw the police rounding up the Jews and assembling them in the center of the marketplace. They entered his sister Pola's home, killing her and throwing her baby girl out the window; her husband escaped. Realizing the man and his son's story was materializing, Samuel snuck out the back door of Fannie's house and into her garden.

Samuel was crouched among the plant stalks when his brother-in-law found him that evening. Avraham was also searching for a safe place to hide from the Gestapo. The two men decided that they had to escape before morning, when the Germans might once again round up the Jews and find them in the process. Unsure if the coast was clear, Avraham offered to depart from the garden first.

"You have a family, and I am single. I'll go out. If you don't hear any shooting, you know it will be safe for you to come too." Avraham ran out from the garden toward the Stubla River. The police opened fire, but he dove under the water before the bullets could catch him and escaped.

Samuel, hearing the gunshots, presumed that Avraham had been killed and that the entire area was under surveillance. Having no means of escape, he stayed in the garden overnight and for much of the next day. On Thursday evening, the local police, likely looking for food to raid, came into the garden and found Samuel lying on the ground. They detained him overnight and on Friday morning forced him, along with more than one hundred other Jewish men, to undress and dance in the street.[1]

After the Germans publicly humiliated them, the Jews were marched to the local cemetery where they were lined up in front of a pit. Lacking enough bullets, the Nazis attempted to kill multiple Jews with one shot, leaving several victims gasping for breath as they slowly suffocated among the discarded bodies of their friends and families.

Once the killing concluded, the Germans promised that there would be no further executions so long as the Jews relocated to a ghetto. The Nazis took over the local pharmacist's house, where Paula's friend Rodel lived, and converted it into the local Gestapo headquarters. From there they sent out the self-appointed police, now formally christened as an arm of the German forces, to paper the village with German signs cataloging an array of new regulations: all Jews in the areas surrounding Serniki were to be brought to the ghetto, any Jews found outside the ghetto perimeter would be shot, Jews were required to wear a yellow star on the front and back of their clothing at all times, Jews were only permitted to walk in the middle of the street and could not use the sidewalks, and Jews were not allowed outside after 5:00 p.m.[2] While non-Jews within the ghetto area did not have to abandon their existing homes, Jews were strictly prohibited from visiting their properties.[3]

The ghetto was overcrowded. All Jews living outside the designated area were forced to relocate into a home that was already occupied by a fellow Jew. The Silberfarb home fell outside the ghetto terrain, and Lea moved into the Shidovitch family's house, bringing along her children, her mother Beyle, and siblings Miashke and Avraham.

Jewish men in the Serniki ghetto were assigned to a daily work detail by the local police, typically digging drainage ditches to prevent the streets from turning to mud and impeding German trucks. As a skilled carpenter, Avraham received special dispensation to continue serving non-Jews in Serniki outside the ghetto. He spent his days working for his once fellow citizens, receiving in exchange small quantities of bread and potatoes that he saved to feed his mother, sister, nieces, and nephew.

As a woman, Lea was ineligible for a work detail that would have afforded her a minuscule amount of food and water, and Bernie was considered too young. Lea crafted whatever trace amounts of food her brother acquired into meals—typically soups made of mostly water and a few potatoes—to sustain the family.

The Silberfarbs tried to live as ordinary a life as possible under the circumstances. Paula learned to crochet, disassembling tattered sweaters for yarn. Lacking electricity, on winter nights she sat curled up by the window, using the light from the moon's reflection on the snow to read whatever books she found lying around the house. Despite the chaos that surrounded her, Paula grew to think fondly of the quiet mornings and nights she spent peering out that window.

Beyle fell ill. Without proper medical care or food, the elderly woman's condition deteriorated rapidly. Wanting to fulfill Beyle's dying wish of seeing her daughters married, the Silberfarbs constructed a makeshift *chuppah* at the foot of Beyle's bed. Though they could not find a rabbi to officiate, Miashke and her partner, Chaim Leib Koifman, exchanged vows in a brief bedside ceremony. Hours later, Beyle was dead.

As time wore on, the situation worsened. Paula was forced to dig drainage ditches on the side of the road, and rumors percolated of an impending *aktion*. Lea, aware that death could befall them any day, decided that they needed to escape. She snuck her family out from the ghetto and into Schlenke's abandoned house, which was close to the river and the old wooden bridge that connected Serniki to what was known in Yiddish as *di naye dorf* (the new village).

Di naye dorf was a wealthy neighborhood on the other side of the river, filled with new homes that abutted the woods. Though the area was outside the Serniki ghetto, the local police and Germans accepted bribes from a few Jewish families who were permitted to remain in their homes. The *di naye dorf* Jews were disconnected from ghetto Jews, who were not permitted to travel to the neighborhood. A local policeman, armed with a gun, stood guard on the bridge to prevent any travel between central Serniki and *di naye dorf*.

The Silberfarbs had a cousin living in *di naye dorf*. Lea was determined to bring her family to that house, where they would be mere steps from the cover of tall fields and near to the forest. Lea could see the foot of the bridge from Schlenke's house and began observing the policeman's patterns. She kept track of his movements and when the bridge was left unguarded for a few minutes during a change of shift or bathroom break.

One Sunday afternoon, Lea waited until she saw the guard leave his post and sent Bernie, Miashke, Chaim, and Chaim's mother and sister running across the bridge. When the guard disappeared again later that evening, Lea, Avraham, Paula, and Sophia made the same trip to *di naye dorf*, carrying only small bags with a change of clothing and a few pieces of bread.

When the latter group reached Lea's cousin's home in *di naye dorf*, it was greeted with reluctance. The house was already packed with people and short on food. Lea was told that Bernie and the Koifmans had stopped by earlier but fled to the woods shortly thereafter. Lea, unsure of where to go next, decided to at least spend the night in *di naye dorf* before traveling onward.

A few hours later, there was a knock on the door. The head of the Serniki *Judenrat* had come to tell them that all Jews were ordered to report to Vysots'k for registration on Wednesday. Though Vysots'k was a long walk—roughly thirty kilometers away

—the Jews in the ghetto rejoiced. A Wednesday registration meant that they were at least going to be kept alive for Monday and Tuesday; it was the closest to safe they had felt since the Nazis invaded.

In light of the news, Lea's cousin tried to convince her that she, her daughters, and Avraham should return to Schlenke's house. "You'll be safe until Wednesday and have better access to food for the next few days from there."

Lea refused, "We're here already. We're not risking going back."

Over his sister's objections, Avraham volunteered to return to Schlenke's house where he could safeguard the contents of the home.

"Who cares about the contents," Lea exclaimed. "Your life is more important!" She was on the verge of tears, pleading with her brother to stay in *di naye dorf*.

"Don't worry," Avraham said, dismissing the concerns. "I'm strong. If something happens during the night I can swim across the river. You stay here with the kids." That evening, he snuck back across the bridge.

As night set in, the six or so families in the *di naye dorf* home fell into deep slumbers. The Jews had been sleeping with one eye open for weeks, paralyzed by the core-shaking anxiety that the Nazis would barge in at any moment to transport them to work camps or worse. But while others relaxed, Lea remained restless. She sat by the window, peering out on the quiet street for hours.

In the dead of night, as her tired eyelids began to sag, Lea was jolted awake by two blinding lights. She noticed more headlights, materializing in the distance. The only time a car had previously entered Serniki at night was about a year prior, when the Gestapo officers came to shoot the 121 Jews.

Panicked, Lea ran around the home, rousing everyone. While the rest of Serniki slept, the houseful of people fled out the back door and dissolved into a field. By the time Lea and her daughters had reached the woods, they could hear the gunfire echoing from Serniki.

9

When the Bakszts snuck back into Iwje in early January 1943, they discovered that they were not the only ones who had given up hope of flight. The Germans sent word to the recently escaped Iwjeans that there would be no consequences if they returned, and many turned back after hearing about the brutal massacre at the farmhouses or realizing just how bleak life was in the frozen woods.[1] But the Nazis were just biding their time. They abandoned the December 31, 1942 raid, waiting to strike when the ghetto was better populated.

It was no secret that an *aktion* was still imminent. During the first two weeks of 1943, fearful Iwje Jews began spending nights hidden in makeshift bunkers. Berko, believing the ghetto to be unsafe, kept his immediate family and Rochel's sister's family inside the factory. He continued to produce leather as usual, providing him with currency to keep the Nazis at bay and feed the nine mouths hidden in the attic. Berko also smuggled food into the ghetto for his step-brother Samson and Samson's wife and baby boy.

On January 20, 1943, the Germans liquidated the Iwje ghetto.[2] They marched the entire Jewish population to Gav'ya, a small town about ten kilometers away.[3] As the Jews were led from the ghetto, local Poles lined the sidewalks jeering at their former neighbors.[4] From Gav'ya 1,110 Jews were transferred to Borisov,[5] including two of Alter Gershovitz's sons and their families,[6] where they died, likely shot in the peat bogs of Biała Bołota in March 1943.[7] A few lucky survivors were transferred to a work camp in Lida.[8] The *shtetl* Iwje was declared *Judenrein* (Jew free).[9]

Of the 4,000 Jews living in Iwje at the turn of the decade, only seventeen remained. All of them worked in Berko's leather factory. The group included Berko, Rochel, David, Batya, Gussie, Samson, and Rochel's sister and her family. Samson's wife and infant son were transported to Borisov. When Berko went to look for his mother-in-law in the vacant ghetto later that night, he found Chana shot dead on the floor of her son's house. Bodies were strewn about the town. Two women who tried to escape lay dead and bloodied against the ghetto fence, their hands still grasping the barbed wire.

The Nazis knew Berko was still in the factory with his family, but given the high value of leather, they allowed him to continue operating with the aid of the few remaining Jews. They assigned them to a home near to the factory and within eyeshot of the local police headquarters and ordered the Jews to stay there when not at work.

Berko understood that the salvation was temporary. He reasoned that his family would have a better chance of survival if they split up, potentially offering at least some of the Bakszts an opportunity to escape into the woods, when necessary. With leather in hand, he visited a local non-Jew with whom he was acquainted to arrange a hiding place for some of his family.

The local man agreed to take in the Bakszt family members and dug a bunker underneath the floor of his barn. The hole was covered with wooden planks that matched the barn floor, though one plank was slightly too short, leaving a small gap between it and the next. The farmer covered the barn floor with a thin layer of hay to mask the hole. The plan was that Rochel, Gussie, and Rochel's sister and her immediate family would stay in the bunker, a total of six people. Berko would periodically drop off leather to compensate the barn owner and food obtained from local farmers to sustain the family.

Back at the house, Berko, David, Samson, and the other workers continued to labor in the factory. Batya, the only woman, was tasked with running the household. She spent most of her time cooking, cleaning, and washing clothes. On days when she finished early, Batya reported to the factory to help with the leathermaking.

Across the street from the factory lived a Polish shoemaker. The man had access to a radio and newspapers, and David would occasionally stop in to ask for updates about the war. While the man was somewhat reluctant to let the Jewish boy inside, he tolerated the visits, likely out of a combination of sympathy and a desire for the free leather he received from the Bakstzts. The news reports kept David and Berko faithful that the Allies would eventually reach them, though they doubted whether they personally would live to see the day.

On rare occasions, Berko, David, and Batya visited the barn at night to see their family. The visits were risky, jeopardizing everyone's safety, and thus kept brief and infrequent. In mid-April, toward the end of Passover, the three Bakszts snuck into the barn to see their family. Able to hug his mother and little sister for the first time in several weeks, David felt comforted.

Two weeks later, on May 8, 1943, three Germans entered the barn. Someone—perhaps a police officer or nosy neighbor—had noticed Berko's periodic visits to the Polish man's home and raised suspicions that Jews may be hiding nearby. The barn was quiet as the Germans walked through, seeing nothing of note. But one German happened to step directly on the gap in the floorboards covering the bunker where the planks were too short to meet. The sparse coating of hay was not enough to support the officer's weight, and the heel of his boot slipped through the hole, landing squarely on the head of one of the hidden Jews.

The German pulled out a hand grenade and dropped it inside the hole. One of David's cousins grabbed it and threw it back out. The grenade exploded, killing one of the Germans and injuring the other two. Gunshots ensued. The two cousins, armed with rifles, jumped out of the bunker to defend their family, but they were quickly shot dead. The Germans then lit the barn on fire, burning the remaining family members alive. The farmer fled, aware that he too would be killed if caught by the authorities. One of his neighbors sent word to Berko.

10

In June 1943, Berko visited with a local farmer to obtain more food. "I'm not supposed to tell you this," the farmer warned. "But the Germans are going to annihilate the Jews." The farmer told Berko that he had heard that the German officers were preparing to surround the factory and kill the remaining workers. He suggested that Berko and his family would be wise to run away and save themselves.

Berko passed the news on to his workforce. He advised his stepbrother to escape to the woods, but Samson refused, holding out hope that one day his wife and child would be returned from Borisov. Samson worried that if he escaped, the Nazis would retaliate against his family. Berko did not have the heart to tell Samson that his family was almost certainly already dead; the Nazis had no use for a woman and a baby.

Shortly thereafter, Berko pulled David and Batya aside. He told them to avoid the factory and that he too was going to spend his time outside under the guise of searching for production materials. "I have a hiding place ready for us." In hushed tones, Berko explained that he had paid off a Polish man living near the factory to take them in when needed. "If something happens," he instructed, "run away and meet me there."

One summer morning, around 8:30 a.m., Berko was out gathering supplies. Bayta was tending to housework in the assigned home, and David had wandered off to visit with the shoemaker across the street from the factory. The two were talking about the war when suddenly the shoemaker jumped up. "Look at that!" he exclaimed, pointing to the window. "Your factory is surrounded!"

There was no good exit option. The front door of the shoemaker's home directly faced the factory, and the small side door was still within eyeshot of the Nazis. The man gave David a jacket to cover the yellow stars on both sides of his shirt. David, determined to meet his father at the rendezvous point, took a deep breath and dashed out the side door.

The Nazi officers surrounding the leather factory noticed David, and two soldiers gave chase. David sprinted down an alley. He could hear gunshots firing behind him. Expecting to feel the sting of the metal piercing his skin at any moment, David remembered being told that he should run in a zigzag pattern if he ever found himself being shot at by the Germans. David began darting between the left and right as he ran, dropping low to the ground every few feet. The bullets missed him.

David escaped his tails and made it to the Polish man's home unscathed. He found his father waiting there for him with a look of despair on his face.

"The Germans surrounded the factory and the house," Berko said. "They took Batya. I have to go back. I have to give myself up," he insisted. "Otherwise they'll kill my daughter."

David stood shocked, out of breath and out of words. He understood that his sister was likely bound for death, if it had not already found her, and he did not know how to explain to his devastated father that they could not go after her. "Dad, if you go back, you are going to do them a favor. They're going to kill you. And if I go, they'll kill me too." David paused, his voice breaking. "What good is it?"

The tears welling in Berko's eyes were rapidly spilling over. "I am a father. I have to do it!" he cried.

"But you are a father to me too," David insisted, beating his chest in anguish. "I don't want to die!"

David, on his knees, begged his father to take him to the partisans instead. It was the only means of keeping themselves alive and having even a chance of rescuing Batya. After several minutes of pleading, Berko acquiesced.

David and Berko knew that they could not stay at the Polish man's house. It was too close to the factory, and there was a risk that they were followed or noticed by the neighbors on their way inside. But establishing contact with the partisans could not be done overnight, and there was no guarantee that a resistance group would even accept them. Though Bielski's Otriad welcomed all, the group had since relocated, and the remaining partisans operating in the area were Soviet fighter units. The Soviets were discerning as to whom they allowed to join their ranks, and Berko and David were Jews with no weapons to contribute.

Berko had heard rumors that another Jewish family was hiding in the barn of an associate about eight kilometers outside of Iwje. He and David decided that the safest option would be to seek temporary shelter there until they could make concrete plans to relocate to the woods. Shortly after sunset, they made their way through the forest to the address.

When they arrived, the owner took David and Berko out back to a barn filled with pigs. The overwhelming scent of manure and ring of buzzing flies was disorienting. Pushing away the animals and hay on the ground, the owner opened a hatch in the floor, revealing a small crawlspace similar to the one in which Rochel and Gussie had been hiding. The bunker was stuffed with people, packed so tightly that they lacked the room to even lift their arms away from their torsos. Despite the unbearably tight quarters, everyone agreed that David and Berko could stay.

David and Berko squeezed into the bunker, somehow finding room in the non-existent space. It was too shallow to stand and too cramped to sit up in. The Jews spent day and night lying flat in the dark, many literally on top of another. At night, David climbed out and sat quietly outside, desperate to flex his stiffening joints and breathe the fresh air.

With the help of the barn owner, Berko was able to make contact with Motke Ginsburg, a young Jewish man he knew from Iwje. Motke had escaped the Iwje ghetto and joined the Soviet Iskra Partisans in the group's early days, bringing guns as a membership offering.[1] Notwithstanding his Jewishness, Motke established himself as an esteemed member of Iskra.[2] He played vital roles in several successful sabotage missions against the Germans and climbed the ranks of the Otriad.[3]

Motke went to bat for Berko and David. He told the Otriad leadership that though they did not have weapons, David was young and able to fight and Berko could produce leather for the group. The promise of a leathermaker tipped the scales. The Iskra Otriad agreed to take in the two new members.

After spending approximately two weeks in the bunker, Berko and David, with the aid of Motke, left for the Naliboki Forest. They walked through the night, following along the Neman River, until they reached the group. Iskra was a partisan unit operating in the same region as Bielski's Jewish Partisans, periodically interacting, but with a radically different philosophy. The unit was filled with physically fit young men, with an occasional nurse or other skilled worker joining the ranks. Many husbands were offered membership into Iskra only to have their wives and children sent to the Bielski Otriad instead.[4] Iskra was almost entirely non-Jewish, primarily composed of Soviet soldiers who had been forced from their posts by the Germans, but also included fighters from pre-war Ukraine and Poland.

Though initially small and informal, the Iskra Otriad grew to accommodate more than 200 members by the time Berko and David arrived. It was commandeered by Joseph Stalin into a formal anti-German unit during the prior winter, when the Soviets installed a new commandant and parachuted in men to train the guerrilla group.[5] Iskra was consolidated into a greater network of thousands of Soviet resistors who dominated large swaths of Poland's forests.[6]

The Iskra Otriad ran as an independent community, with each member assigned a daily role. Certain partisans were responsible for maintaining the food supply by foraging in the woods and from Polish locals in nearby towns. Their spoils were brought back to the cooks who prepared and disseminated meals three times each day. There was a medical unit, where a few doctors and nurses provided care to sick or injured members using whatever medicine could be scoured from the forest or pilfered from peasants and Germans.[7] Another group of men were tasked with liaising with Moscow. They received updates on the war effort and upcoming missions as well as swapped intelligence about enemy movements. The partisans also coordinated air drops with the Soviet Union, which dumped crucial supplies and weapons deep in the forest near partisan signal fires.

Many Iskra men served as fighters. Some stood guard around the perimeter of the camp, watching for intruders. A skilled subset built weaponry, repurposing rifles into machine guns using springs made from car tire wire and guns from abandoned Soviet tanks.[8] The remainder were sent on near-daily diversionary missions to disrupt Nazi operations and steal German supplies and weapons.

Berko and David were immediately thrown into their assignments. Berko was offered basic supplies and tasked with producing leather for the Soviet fighters. David was handed a gun and given a brief training on how to use it before he was sent out on his first mission.

11

When they reached the woods, the escaped families from the home in *di naye dorf* splintered off. Most were women with husbands and grown children who had friends or business colleagues who could take them in. Despite being the one who had sounded the alarm, within days, Lea found herself abandoned in the woods with two young girls, ages eleven and nine.

Lea remembered that a friend of her late husband lived relatively nearby, on the edge of the woods. Dimitro Lacunyetz was a non-Jewish farmer with whom Samuel had frequently stayed while searching for forest plots to purchase for timber. Lea walked Paula and Sophia through the woods until they reached Dimitro's house.

Lea knocked on Dimitro's door in the middle of the night. So much had changed since she had last seen him, and Lea was not sure how he and his family would react to their impromptu arrival. After the Nazis invaded, many Poles deserted their Jewish friends. Dimitro opened the door, took one look at Lea, Paula, and Sophia, and began to weep. He pulled them inside the house immediately and hugged them tightly. "I was so worried they killed you in Serniki!"

Dimitro said that after they had escaped *di naye dorf*, Bernie led

Miashke, Chaim, and Chaim's family to his home, hoping that Dimitro might be willing to help them. Bernie told Dimitro that his mother and sisters had also escaped, but he was not sure where they had gone. Hours later, Dimitro heard the gunshots coming from Serniki.

Word quickly spread that the Germans had carried out another *aktion*, liquidating Serniki early that morning. The Gestapo, along with Polish and Ukrainian police, stormed the ghetto and dragged Jews from their beds. The Jews were stripped naked and shot into pits by a killing squad. In one day, the entire Jewish population of Serniki— 850 people—was murdered. Dimitro was terrified that Lea and the girls were included in that number.

Dimitro stirred his wife and had her prepare a meal for the Silberfarbs. He noticed that Lea was wincing with each step, struggling to mask the pain of walking. Her feet were bloodied and blistered from running in heels, the only shoes she had with her when she fled *di naye dorf*.

While Lea and her children gobbled down their first proper meal in over a year, Dimitro got to work. He crafted Lea a pair of *kostelez* (homemade shoes), wrapping rags around her feet and encrusting them with woven tree bark tied together with a thin rope. Lea, Paula, and Sophia spent the night in the house.

The next morning, after breakfast, Dimitro took Lea and the girls to meet up with their family whom he had hidden in the woods. The reunion was cheerful, despite the trying conditions. The Silberfarbs escaped death, and though stuck in the forest, they were at least somewhat liberated from the watchful eyes of their German captors.

The group was unfamiliar with the woods and so it stayed put, afraid of running into Nazi collaborators or getting lost in the seemingly endless landscape. Once each day, Dimitro or his son-in-law materialized with food, varying the time and route taken to make the delivery; visiting any more frequently risked attracting unwanted attention.

The daily provisions typically consisted of a kettle filled with potato and millet soup and a single spoon. Lea also smuggled a silver spoon with her, and the group of eight alternated eating from the kettle, two at a time. Notwithstanding Dimitro's generosity, food remained scare, and the group often bickered over portions. "Don't eat too much," they chastised each other. "Leave some for me!"

Not wanting to appear ungrateful, the group made do with whatever it was brought. But after a few days, the Silberfarbs became desperate for drinking water and worked up the courage to ask Dimitro's son-in-law. The man was taken aback; he assumed that the family had been using water from the nearby stream. "Half a kilometer from here there is water," he gestured in the direction of what looked like more forest. "It's safe. You can go and get some." The Lacunyetz family had not realized that the Jews had been too petrified to move from their hiding spot.

Between Dimitro's food supply and the stream, the Silberfarbs carried on in the woods for months. When the weather turned chilly, Dimitro's son-in-law built them a shelter. He tied together the wood from young birch trees and covered the hut in leaves for insulation. Combined with nightly fires, the family kept warm enough.

But the situation was growing increasingly untenable. Dimitro was worried that his son-in-law would turn the Jews in if the right opportunity presented and warned Lea that he could not be trusted. The children were hungry, and Chaim's mother succumbed to the rough conditions.

Bernie decided that he needed to find more food. Over Lea's objections, the thirteen-year-old boy ran away and came across some farmers digging potatoes near the edge of the forest. Bernie asked whether they would share.

"Are you a Jew or a Gypsy?" the farmers asked the dirt-covered boy.

"I am a Gypsy," Bernie said.

Two hours later, Bernie returned to the campsite with a grin and hands filled with bread and baked pumpkin.

A partisan detachment was forming in the forest, just a few kilometers from where the Silberfarbs were hiding. The unit, led by Maxine Misoura, was composed of Jews, Soviets, and locals who opposed Germany's occupation. While Lea knew the partisans would never accept a single woman with three children into their ranks, she understood that hiding in their presence would at least provide some additional security.

Though they lived in the forest, Misoura's partisans relied on the local community for sustenance. Heavily armed, they often asked for, or else stole, food from farmers in the area. One evening in late 1942, a few partisans approached a nearby farm, seeking a cow from the wealthy owner. The farmer's son, unsympathetic to the partisan cause, opened fire on the forest dwellers. The partisans shot back and killed the man. The farmer ran out of his house screaming. He vowed to avenge his son's death, swearing that he would report the whereabouts of those hiding in the nearby forest.

News of the incident spread to other farmers. Dimitro came running to Lea and her family, panicked that the Germans would find them. Convinced that the woods near his home were no longer safe, Dimitro insisted that the Silberfarbs relocate immediately. He was aware of a group of Jews hiding in the woods near Svarytsevych, several kilometers away, living in the shadow of a partisan group. He gave Lea instructions on how to find them and some food scraps to tide them over on the journey. After sixteen weeks of being cared for by Dimitro, the group departed that night.

Lea led the group of seven toward Svarytsevych. It was a chilly winter night, and they had to mind their footprints so as not to leave a trace back to them in the snow. Though the conditions made walking physically difficult for her, Paula was enamored with the peaceful view of snow blanketing the trees. After several hours of travel, they reached their destination.

The Jews in the Svarytsevych Forest had their own camp, adjacent to that of the partisans. The Jewish camp was unaffiliated with the partisan camp, but the partisans' presence indirectly afforded them protection. Some of those in the Jewish camp had relatives in the partisan group who occasionally passed along information and food. Whenever the partisan camp advanced, the Jewish camp invariably trailed behind it.

Lea, unwilling to risk her children's lives any more than

necessary, took upon herself the responsibility of scouring for food. At night, she snuck into the nearby village and begged local farmers for a piece of bread or a potato. The children, meanwhile, waited with bated breath for her return, worried that she stumbled into unfriendly territory or was caught by the police. Many farmers took pity and offered up food. Others shooed Lea away, as if she were garbage. On one occasion, a farmer threatened Lea. "Go away you dirty Jew," he shouted at her, "or I'll call the Germans on you!" Lea took off running.

One night, Lea did not return to the campsite as she usually did. The children lay awake inside their manmade hut all night, fearful and clueless about where to search for her if she did not return by dawn. As daybreak crept through the trees and the birds began to sing, Bernie, Paula, and Sophia finally spotted Lea in the distance, hobbling. As she grew closer, Paula noticed that one of the *kostelez* that Dimitro had made for Lea was shredded, encrusted in dried blood. The children ran to her, and Lea tried to reassure them that she was okay. She explained that a farmer answered her knock on the door by releasing a large dog. The animal charged at her, tearing open her foot with its teeth.

Lea sat down and peeled off the ragged layers of her torn *kostelez*, sticky with blood. They revealed a marred foot, oozing and stinging sharply. On the advice of others in the camp, Paula collected pinecones and boiled them in water, using the brown-stained liquid as a disinfectant. Every day, Lea washed out the wound with the pinecone brew, hoping it would stave off infection.

Though the Jews shared a campsite, they periodically split up into smaller factions at times of perceived heightened risk. Upon hearing increased activity or gunfire in the distance, the Jews scattered, forming pods in their own corners of the forest. Sometimes the commotion would be a false alarm or even positive news. At one point the partisans spooked the Jews, rowdy with excitement about their capture of Daniello Polohovitch, the Serniki local responsible for shooting Gershon and multiple other Jews in town. The partisans had taken it upon themselves to exact revenge, and for days after Polohovitch's death, the hand he had used to shoot his gun sat on a log, detached and on display for the Jewish camp.

When these periods of alarm occurred, Lea found herself abandoned with just her family. Other group members viewed children as a liability and kept their distance from the Silberfarbs. Lea was enraged by the selfishness of leaving a woman crippled by a slow-healing wound with three kids. On one occasion, as everyone began to peel off, she confronted the group. "How could you do this?" she questioned. "We are also Jewish, so what if we joined you?"

But Bernie stopped her from pressing the issue. "Don't beg," he cautioned. "If they don't want us, we are not going to follow them."

Lea watched as the Jews splintered off and disappeared into the woods.

After hiding by themselves for about a week, Lea and the children heard gunfire in the distance. When the sounds eventually dissipated, a few Jews emerged. They explained that much of the group had reassembled farther away, establishing a separate camp. A rogue group of antisemitic fighters had encountered the Jewish sub-group and shot them all dead.

The few remaining members of the Jewish camp reconvened. The partisans were again on the move, bound to join forces with another unit. The Jews had to follow.

12

After rounding up the few remaining workers from Berko's factory in Iwje, the Germans transported them to a work camp near Lida. Lida was a small city about thirty kilometers from Iwje with an alarmingly similar history. The Germans massacred about 2,000 Jews before walling off the remaining survivors into a ghetto that was subsequently liquidated.[1] Of the approximately 8,500 Jews in Lida when the Nazis first invaded, fewer than 300 were still alive.[2]

The Iwje workers slept in barracks inside a jail. The jail was populated by Jews who were apprehended and transported from other ghettos, largely for violating Nazi orders or trying to escape.[3] Each morning the Iwje prisoners were marched from the jail to a large factory, where they were put to work making leather. German officials heavily guarded the area, but the prisoners had some limited freedom of movement within the enclosed vicinity of the factory. The Jews were given a brief respite for lunch—a sliver of bread and some water—and were paraded back to the jail at the end of the day.

One afternoon when Batya was walking near the factory, she heard the thump of something hitting the ground. Looking down, she noticed a package on the ground, oddly shaped and wrapped in cloth. Batya heard a faint sound of whimpering emanating from the package. Thinking it was an abandoned kitten, she bent down and peeled back the fabric.

Batya jumped back startled, confronted with the nearly lifeless face of a newborn baby. She instinctively scooped up the infant who was cold to the touch. The baby was severely malnourished and too weak to let out anything more than a slight fuss. Batya stuffed the baby under her clothes against her warm body and hurried back to the jail. She named the infant Ilana.

Though she lacked any long-term plan, Batya was determined to nurture Ilana back to life. She snuck the baby into the factory with her each day and further starved herself so that she could feed Ilana whatever minimal amounts of water and food she could amass. At night, Batya held the baby against her chest, using her own body heat to keep Ilana warm in the chilly prison. Miraculously, over the course of several days, the baby began to improve.

One night, baby Ilana finally mustered the strength to cry. The sound attracted the attention of a German patrol guard who came inside the barracks to investigate. He found Batya attempting to soothe the baby. The guard ripped Ilana out of Batya's arms and threw the baby to the ground. He plunged his bayonet into the Ilana's whimpering chest, killing her in front of Batya's eyes. Batya shrieked.

In the partisans, David was sent out on his first mission. The unit had obtained intelligence, presumably through local connections or Moscow channels, that German trucks would be traveling along a certain road running through the woods. David, along with several partisan comrades, trekked through the forest on foot until he reached the roadway. The fighters divided themselves into two groups, each assigned to opposite sides of the street. The groups sat down in a row along the roadside, one group positioned about a kilometer farther down from the other. Hidden under the tree cover that abutted the road, the fighters waited for hours, patiently listening for the sound of approaching trucks. Eventually, they heard the roar of engines, and a long line of German vehicles emerged from the distance. The partisans held in place until all the trucks had driven inside the guarded zone. Then they opened fire.

David, on the firing side of a gun for the first time, felt no remorse as he shot at the ambushed soldiers. Surprised by the encounter, most of the Germans were killed on the spot, though a few managed to escape into the woods on foot. Once the Nazis were all dead, sprawled lifelessly on the street and in the trucks, the partisans approached them. After losing most of his family to the Nazis, David was hardened and unfazed as he literally stepped over bloody bodies to reach the trucks. He took pleasure in the vengeance. The partisans looted anything useful for the Iskra stockpile: supplies being transported; ammunition; and guns, many pulled directly off the warm bodies to which they were strapped. Having no use for the trucks themselves, the partisans set them ablaze and returned to camp.

Fortified by weapons and reports of advancing Soviet forces, David finally grew optimistic that he could outlive the Nazis and tell the story of his survival. He and his co-fighters made it their personal mission to exact revenge on the Germans, no matter how demanding the task. They spent every night attacking the enemy, blowing up trains, bridges, trucks, and military outposts. They burned down Nazi warehouses, destroyed steam engines, and killed hundreds of Germans in the process. What the group lacked in might it made up for in scrappiness; operations were carefully plotted to target strategic locations, doing the most damage to communication and transportation infrastructure in the least amount of time. Though intentional direct confrontations were less common, when undertaken, the partisans always sought to benefit from the element of surprise.

Particularly important to David and his peers were the locals who cooperated with partisan efforts. When traveling for missions, the partisans would sometimes stop over at a home, asking for food and shelter. Other times they demanded larger quantities of food from farmers, who were aware that if the harvests were not given to the partisans, the Germans would likely confiscate them anyway.[4] Peasants became critical sources of intelligence and aid, assisting as seemingly innocent third parties in rescue missions and providing information about German movements or plans. The locals complied out of fear if not sympathy. Like the Bielskis, Soviet partisans were known to burn down the homes of those who did not comply with their demands and kill anyone who dared provide the Germans with compromising information.

Even so, there were close calls. The Germans had their own tactics for threatening, if not bribing, locals for intelligence on the partisans. They offered 10,000 Reichsmarks per Iskra scout—delivered dead or alive.[5] There was also an ever-present risk that Nazi forces would ambush the Iskra fighters or engage in retaliatory fire during planned attacks. On more than one occasion, David was shot at by the enemy. Upon emerging from the woods in a nearby town, he found Nazis awaiting his arrival with guns at the ready. He was fortunate to run away into the forest, though many of his peers were killed by gunfire.

Though David understood that his sister had likely been killed by the Germans, he and his father never gave up on trying to locate Batya. Through the partisan network, they eventually learned that the factory workers from Iwje were alive, transported for further work in Lida. Berko was determined to formulate a rescue mission. He made contact with another partisan who was well connected with locals who supported the resistance. The man introduced Berko to Mr. Yankevich, a Polish native who agreed to bring Batya to the partisans in exchange for some gold coins.

Berko gave Mr. Yankevich an envelope. On the outside of the envelope David had written in Yiddish:

My fellow Jews, whoever finds this letter please give it to Batya Bakszt.

Mr. Yankevich dropped the letter by a well where many of the Lida factory workers congregated at lunchtime. Sure enough, a Jew found the letter and handed it off to Batya. Batya was shocked to recognize her brother's handwriting. Inside he had written:

Next week on Wednesday, when you have your lunch at twelve o'clock, a Polish man by the name of Yankevich will come by. Stay and watch for him. He will take you out of there.

The following Wednesday at noon Mr. Yankevich appeared near the factory. Batya was outside with her meager lunch, eyes peeled for someone who also seemed to be subtly searching around. The two made eye contact, and Batya approached him. "Are you Yankevich?" she asked in Polish.

Mr. Yankevich nodded. "Rip off the yellow star from the front of your top. Take me under my arm, my daughter, and walk with me," he whispered.

As Batya yanked off the Star of David from her front, Mr. Yankevich pulled off the one sewed into the back of her shirt and draped a coat over her shoulders to cover the tears. Batya hugged Mr. Yankevich's arm tightly, as if he was endeared to her. In actuality, he was keeping the young woman steady, her body trembling with nerves.

The pair walked down the heavily patrolled street without issue until they reached a German checkpoint. Batya looked on anxiously as Mr. Yankevich calmly produced several pieces of paper from his breast pocket and handed them to a German guard. Unbeknownst to Batya, the guard had already been bribed. After reviewing the falsified documents attesting to their relationship and non-Jewish ancestry, the official waived them through. Mr. Yankevich and Batya walked out of the prison grounds, the Nazis fading into the distance behind them.

Mr. Yankevich took Batya to a home on the outskirts of Lida that belonged to his sister. The two rested until nightfall, when it was safe to resume their journey to the Iskra camp. They trekked through the forest all night, while David and Berko waited up anxiously. At 5:00 a.m. the following morning, they reached the partisan camp.

The reunion was overwhelming. Berko and David began sobbing upon seeing Batya emerge through the trees, almost unable to believe their own eyes. They considered it a miracle that she was safely returned to them. After giving his sister a tight hug, David turned to his father. "See dad," he said, "it's a good thing we didn't go to the Germans after all."

Berko put his arm around David and planted a kiss on his cheek. For the first time in years, they felt happiness.

13

Lea was sitting with her children in the square of a small partisan-friendly village near Vychivka. The Jewish camp was wrapping up a brief rest and preparing to continue onward in their pursuit of the relocating partisans. Lea stood up and immediately collapsed in pain, her foot unable to support her weight. Though she tried with all her strength, Lea's foot refused to move, sore and still hobbled by her injury. "It's okay, it's okay, you go with the camp," Lea assured her three children. "I'll rest up here, and then I'll come find you."

Sophia started to cry. "I'm not going without you!"

"Don't worry, I'll find you," Lea insisted.

As Sophia grew more distraught, Bernie let out an exasperated huff. "What is the matter with you?" he asked his mother. "All this time you were fine, and now, when it's so crucial, you get sick? I don't want to die because of you." Bernie was eager to continue on with the rest of the camp.

"If the girls are not going, you need to stay too," Lea explained to Bernie. "I can't move. I need you to make a fire and tend to them."

Several homes lined the square that surrounded them, all seemingly left deserted after the Germans invaded. Lea pointed to one, proposing that the four of them seek shelter inside.

"I'm not coming," Bernie announced. He watched Paula and Sophia help Lea into the house, turned around, and left.

Upon entering the home, Lea noticed a deep brick oven with a bowl of rising dough sitting atop it. She realized that someone would be back to bake bread and hoped that when they did, they would prove sympathetic to her and the girls. In the meantime, Lea, Paula, and Sophia rested.

A couple of hours later, they heard the door creek open. Lea, thinking it was the home's owner, took a deep breath and prepared herself for a potential confrontation. Then she heard a familiar voice.

"Mommy?" Bernie's head peaked through the cracked-open doorway. "I couldn't go away and leave you alone," he cried as he scurried inside. "I just couldn't, so I had to come back!" Lea squeezed Bernie tightly, deeply relieved.

Later that day, the owner, a local farmer, returned. He found Lea desperately begging him to help save her three children. "It's okay," he reassured her. The owner explained that he himself was a partisan supporter and, like many locals, was sleeping in the forest with his family to keep themselves safe. He told Lea that she and the children could stay in his hut, which was recently vacated after his family had decided to relocate deeper inside the woods. He led them into the forest to a small wooden structure.

In exchange for food, Lea offered to mend clothes for the kind farmer. The Silberfarbs fell into a daily routine. The farmer brought Lea a steady supply of food and villagers' clothing for repair. Lea spent her day sewing up holes in worn shirts and pants, no longer acutely concerned about where to find the children their next meal.

Though she still worried that the Germans or local police would raid the forest, Lea masked her fears of discovery well and encouraged her children to enjoy the wilderness. Paula, now twelve, passed the time appreciating the serenity of her surroundings. She felt safe in the woods, watching the ever-reliable sun travel across the sky each day.

After about six weeks, Lea recovered from her injury. Though the arrangement with the farmer was beneficial, Lea still believed that her children would be safer hiding in the shadow of a formal partisan brigade. She asked the farmer if there were any otriads operating within walking distance, and he advised her to travel onward to Vychivka, where they could reunite with the Jewish camp that they were with previously.

On the morning of their planned departure, Lea roused her children as she finished the last-minute preparations for their journey. Suddenly, they heard the spit of gunfire in the distance. It was coming from the direction of Vychivka. Lea, aware that the farmer likely also had heard the noise, decided to stay hidden in the hut until he returned with an explanation.

Sure enough, the farmer resurfaced. He explained that the partisans in Vychivka had grown overconfident and drank excessively the prior night. A rogue group of Crimeans ambushed the partisans in the morning, killing many in the adjacent Jewish camp. Now out of alternative options, Lea decided to stay in the hut for the time being.

About a week later, the farmer came running. "There is a man on a horse in the square," he said. "He heard there were Jews hiding nearby and wants to see you." The farmer did not know the man's name but assured Lea that he was not a German.

Lea, skeptical that the man was truly harmless, paused for a moment. "Okay," she said. "Kids, you stay here, and I'm going to go and meet him."

Bernie, Paula, and Sophia all refused to allow their mother to go into the open square alone. Unable to convince them otherwise, Lea agreed that all four of them would meet the visitor.

As they entered the square, they immediately recognized the man atop the horse. "Matis!" Lea greeted him warmly. Matis Bubrov was the father of Chaiah, Paula's childhood playmate. His entire family—four children and his wife—had been murdered by the Nazis in the Serniki ghetto mere days before *Rosh Hashanah*, the Jewish new year, in 1942. Matis had escaped to the woods. He had heard rumors of a Jewish family in the area and came to offer directions to a Jewish camp, not realizing that they were his former neighbors. After a brief but joyful reunion, Matis gave Sophia his coat and Lea instructions to locate another Jewish camp near the partisans in Lasitsk,[1] about twenty kilometers away.

After saying goodbye to the farmer, the Silberfarbs proceeded onward. The walk was lengthy, and the children grew weary. Often they complained, afraid to be all alone in the forest and at constant risk of discovery by the Nazis or local police.

Lea patiently combated their anxiety with words of encouragement. "Shh, the war will finish," she assured them. "We are going to be free soon."

Paula, unable to comprehend a world beyond Serniki and the vast surrounding forest, was confused. "But there are no more Jewish people left in the world!" she responded.

Lea kept the children occupied as they walked, telling stories of their Jewish family in Cuba and Brazil whom they would visit one day soon. Sophia's imagination filed with pictures of beaches and palm trees, landscapes that she had never seen in person. "We also can stay with Hashke Neiditz, my old teacher, in Canada," Paula would occasionally recall.

They reached the Jewish camp. The camaraderie was reassuring, but conditions were nonetheless brutal. During the winter they huddled together to keep warm, unequipped with proper cold-weather attire. Lea continued to beg for food, aided by the children who dug beneath the snow, scavenging for berries. In warmer weather, they slept directly under the stars. One night Paula awoke to find herself completely covered in snakes attracted to her body heat. Petrified that they would bite her, Paula lay motionless for hours until the sun came up and they slithered away.

Though Lea and her children were perceived as a burden in their prior camp, in the Lasitsk camp babies were the bigger concern. Their need for food and uncontrollable cries made them a liability. Mothers of young children received wayward glances and icy treatment, which escalated into clear contempt as German forces became more prevalent in the area.

Discovery was a death sentence for everyone, but the Nazis were particularly vicious to babies. They were known to force women to hold their infants against their chests, shooting through the baby's head and into the mother's heart in a single shot to conserve bullets. Other times, the Germans tortured the mother by swinging her baby by the legs until its head was split open on a tree trunk as she looked on. When a mother with twins was discovered near the camp, a German grabbed one infant in each hand, clapping their heads together like a cymbal.

One day, a baby in the camp would not stop crying. The group was not far from the edge of the woods in an area that the Nazis were patrolling. The mother, a woman named Bashke Fialkov, struggled to quell the hungry child. Bashke was widowed in Serniki, left to care for three young children on her own. Her youngest's cries had already garnered her threats of excommunication from the group, and looks of panic set in as the infant's wails threatened to give away the group's hiding spot. Bashke, desperate to keep her other daughters and fellow Jews alive, covered the crying baby's nose and mouth with her hand. After a minute the baby grew quiet and shortly thereafter went limp.

Over a series of months, the Jewish camp trailed the partisans' movements, wandering about the modern-day border region of Ukraine and Belarus. Some villages were friendly, identifying overwhelmingly with the resistance and offering food and supplies. Others less so, filled with Nazi sympathizers or German military officials. Relatively sheltered from such threats in the woods, Paula and Sophia remained somewhat ignorant to just how acute the situation was around them. Lea did her best to keep it that way.

In one unfriendly territory, Lea was walking near the edge of the forest searching for food when she spotted a Nazi soldier. Separated only by an open plain, the two locked eyes, pausing as if to make sure the other was not a mirage. The soldier slowly lifted his rifle and took aim at Lea. With nowhere to hide, Lea turned her back on the Nazi and began retreating toward the woods. As she took a few steps, Lea worried what fate would befall her children in her absence. She braced herself for the pierce of the bullet, knowing the Nazi had a clean shot. The bullet never came.

14

Batya was adopted into Iskra. She was tasked with cooking for the unit, finding ways to craft three meals a day from whatever food could be located. Mostly the group lived off a combination of potatoes and water. On good days, someone would steal some beans or even meat from a farmer. On bad ones, the group was left with nothing to eat but snow. On one occasion, the partisans somehow obtained horse meat, which Batya did her best to cook. The Jews, desperate for nourishment, swallowed the non-kosher meat with disgust.

There were few girls in Iskra, which left sixteen-year-old Batya particularly vulnerable. The young women who were accepted often relied on men for protection. It was common for a young partisan woman to pair up with a man early on, implicitly trading sex for the extra clothing or food he would sneak back from missions. With Berko and David looking out for her, Batya was fortunate to not be placed in such a position. Nevertheless, she still felt a sense of obligation to Fishel Bialobroda.

Fishel was an Iskra partisan about eight years Batya's senior. He had seen his own share of horrors in occupied Poland. Before escaping to the partisans, Fishel had been selected for death in a

Nazi *aktion* in Lida. He was shot into a pit with thousands of other Jews after attempting to hide in a pile of clothing stripped from the victims. Despite being shot in the spine, Fishel managed to escape from the pit and ensuing gunfire. Though his injuries were serious, he ultimately recovered, fueled in the first few days by eating a rotten potato and drinking his own brother's urine.[1] The injury left him permanently branded with a Frankenstein-like scar across his abdomen.

Aside from trauma, Batya and Fishel had little in common. One of eleven children, Fishel had grown up poor and worked as a barber in Warsaw and Lida prior to the war. He was a rough-and-tumble man who had rightly earned a reputation as being willing to do anything for a few złoty. As a partisan, he served in a combat role, attacking Germans and killing locals who sabotaged the group. In any other world, highbrowed Batya would have no interest in Fishel. But he played a role in coordinating her rescue from the Lida jail,[2] and Batya felt indebted to him. They began dating over Berko's firm objections.

Meanwhile, David continued carrying out missions. He received regular updates on the progress of the war and the advancing Eastern Front. David was focused on blowing up trains heading to the battlefield with supplies. His unit would obtain or make explosives, often repurposed hand grenades, and lay them on train tracks that ran through the woods. The explosives were attached to a string that led from the tracks into the forest. When a train traversed the area of the track with the bomb, David, hidden in the woods with his comrades, pulled the string and fled. The explosion derailed the trains and brought transit along that route to a halt.

After one mission, an Iskra fighter approached Berko with news. Mr. Yankevich had been killed in his home by the partisans. "Why would you do that?" Berko asked. The partisan explained that, through local intelligence, they had discovered that the man who had rescued Batya was a double agent enlisted by the Germans to sabotage partisan activities. The explanation did not make sense to Berko. "What do you mean? He saved my daughter."

Mr. Yankevich had saved Batya to earn Iskra's trust. His plan was to ingratiate himself with the group by saving the girl and become privy to more valuable information that could be passed along to the Nazis.

Daily life remained largely stable as winter approached, but the cold weather exacerbated existing challenges. Temperatures dropped well below freezing for much of January through March 1944. Heavy snow and whiteout conditions afforded greater protection from German forces who increasingly sought to dampen the growing partisan threat. But snow prints also left easy clues to the partisans' whereabouts, and the fighters had to be continually mindful of their motions—walking backward or sending out men to create diversionary paths in the snow.

Sleeping outside, as was done in the summertime, meant freezing to death, so the group built discreet underground shelters. These *zemlyankas* (Russian for dugouts) were made by digging large holes into the ground and constructing walls and roofs from dirt, brush, and trees.[3] The process was time consuming and labor intensive, made worse by the need to dispose of unused materials, like the displaced soil, several kilometers away so as not to compromise their location if noticed.[4]

At night, the partisans packed tightly inside the *zemlyankas*, using their bodies and a small wood-burning furnace for warmth. The shelters helped, but frostbite remained common, and the combination of cold and wet created a hotbed for gangrene. One cold day, Batya undid her shoelaces and pulled out her foot. It immediately swelled up so large that she could not get it back inside the shoe. She never took her shoes off again for the rest of that winter.

On quiet days, Batya sometimes snuck away from the camp for a walk. She never ventured too far, staying within the guarded perimeter, but the solitude provided a brief respite. While walking, she noticed a Torah on the ground. It was a smaller version than those typically used in synagogues, sized for a children's service and missing the decorative cover that protects the scroll. Batya was unsure what to do with it. It would not be a welcomed possession in the mostly Soviet camp that barely tolerated Jews, but she could not leave the holy item in the dirt; Torah scrolls are considered so sacred in the Jewish faith that it customary for anyone who witnesses one dropped on the ground to fast for forty days.

Batya swept up the Torah and took it with her. It was marred by dirt and smelled of charcoal, rescued from a burning synagogue she suspected. Using whatever materials she could find, Batya made a protective cover for it and kept the Torah safely hidden with her in the woods. Whenever the group relocated, Batya hid the scroll under her clothing, pressing it against her chest or stomach as if she were pregnant.[5]

As news continued to flood in about the advancing war efforts, the Bakszts knew that liberation was just a matter of time. They followed the freeing of Leningrad, the Allied Forces' arrival at Normandy, and the Soviet Army's advances in the east. One July morning, in 1944, the partisans finally received the radio call that the Soviets had arrived. All partisans operating in the nearby forests were commanded to report to Lida. Over 200 Iskra fighters made their way to the town's marketplace.

The marketplace was flooded with partisans, guns in tow. The local military leadership organized a joyous parade, with speeches commending the forest fighters for their efforts on behalf of the Motherland. Whatever resentment the Bakszts had held against the Soviets for their invasion of Iwje had thawed; the Soviet partisans protected them from the Nazis, and the Red Army liberated them. They were free. Berko, David, Batya—with Fishel and her Torah in tow—embraced, crying bittersweet tears. The Bakszts did not know where their next stop would be, but they were finally unburdened of the constant fear that they would be captured and killed by German forces.

As they stood there in the market rejoicing, Red Army soldiers began wading through the crowd, looking over the men. "You're coming to the Army," one said to David.

The look on Berko's face turned from elation to terror. "Please," Berko began to cry. "This is the only son I have left. We just went through hell. They killed everyone. Please, let my son stay here with me."

Berko's pleas fell on deaf ears. "Don't worry," the Soviet soldier said, pulling David away. "He's not going to the front to fight. We will send him to school to be a sergeant."

15

In late fall 1943, the partisans led the Silberfarbs to Nen'kovychi, a village on the Hnyla Lypa River, northwest of Serniki. The residents of Nen'kovychi were largely supporters of the partisans and generous to the poor Jews begging for supplies. While seeking food, Lea encountered a sympathetic farmer whose son had left to join the partisans. He offered food and shelter to her and her children in exchange for help around the property. Lea, thrilled to find an indoor haven for her children, agreed.

The lady of the house asked Lea if Paula could crochet a scarf for her. Before Paula had an opportunity to interject, Lea responded. "Yes, she knows how to do it."

The lady went off to retrieve supplies while panic set in on Paula's face. "Mommy," she exclaimed, "I've never made something like that!"

Lea tried to calm her daughter. "But you know how to crochet from the ghetto," Lea responded. "You can figure it out."

The lady came back with an oversized scarf made by a Jewish girl who was hidden in a nearby barn with another family. Taking cues from her mother, Paula agreed to make the scarf. Pleased with the arrangement, the lady insisted that Paula come live inside the main house, where she could crochet more easily, while the others stayed in the barn.

Inside the house, Paula was treated well. She was invited to eat at the table with the farmer and his wife, who served her three proper meals each day. Having spent months eating whatever could be scavenged in the forest like an animal, Paula found the return to normalcy jarring. She crocheted from early morning until late at night without complaint, using thin yarn that the lady made from flax seed. The house lacked electricity, so Paula burned small pieces of pine wood for light.

After weeks of trial and error, Paula successfully finished the scarf, a roughly yard-and-a-half-sized square with scalloped edges all around. Satisfied with Paula's work, the lady enlisted Paula to crochet smaller woolen items for her son and his peers in the partisans. Paula spent the winter making wool socks and mittens with two separate finger pockets so the wearer could readily operate a gun.

The farmer's neighbors and friends were partisan supporters, but out of an abundance of caution, Paula was still sent out to the barn whenever he had company over. There, Lea, Bernie, and Sophia were well fed and sheltered from the winter. During the day, they helped with chores around the house and property. Lea frequently baked bread to feed the forest fighters.

As the chill of winter began to dissipate, the partisans in the area received good news from Moscow. The Soviet forces continued to advance as the Germans retreated. They were told that Rafalivka, a town about sixty kilometers south of Nen'kovychi, had been liberated. The partisans and the Jewish camp that the Silberfarbs came from decided to make their way to Rafalivka, chasing the nearby promise of freedom. The Silberfarbs joined, and so began a multi-week trek.

Back with the Jewish camp, Lea reunited with her sister and brother-in-law, Miashke and Chaim. The group only walked in the forest, elongating the journey but offering greater protection and the ability to travel during daylight hours. At night, they set up camp in the woods and slept. As they drew closer to Rafalivka, the travelers heard rustling. Then, they spotted a pack of soldiers in the distance. Unsure whether the military presence was friend or foe, a few partisans approached, guns drawn. Shortly thereafter the partisans gave the all-clear sign. The military men were from the Red Army.

The Jewish camp rejoiced. The Soviet soldiers greeted the tired but jubilant Jews and partisans with offerings of canned goods, chocolate, and cigarettes. They celebrated their liberation in the woods before continuing onward to Rafalivka.

When the Silberfarbs reached Rafalivka, they found it occupied by the Soviets. The Red Army soldiers immediately noticed Chaim, a young, fit man, and sent him to the train station to be drafted into the military. Rafalivka's train station made it a notable transportation holding for the Soviets, a target of the Germans, and from Paula's perspective, a major urban environment.

The excitement of arrival was quickly interrupted by the sounds of warplanes above. Suddenly, the sky was darkened by *Luftwaffe* planes dropping bombs. As smoke filled the streets and the sounds of explosions reverberated, the Silberfarbs and their fellow Jews ran for cover. They crammed into several houses on an abandoned street, once home to Jews killed or transported by the Germans.

When the bombings finally stopped, Lea looked around for her children, assuming they would be hysterical. But Sophia was nowhere to be found. In the chaos, they were somehow unwittingly separated. Lea ran outside, going house to house frantically searching for her daughter. With no luck, Lea began interrogating the people emerging into the street. "Have you seen a little girl? Nine years old?" A few remarked that they had noticed a child without a dress on, running around in only thermal underwear. After following similar leads around the neighborhood, Lea eventually found Sophia, indeed bearing nothing but her undergarments and with no explanation.

Lea relocated her children and Miashke to another section in the town, hoping that they would be less vulnerable to bombings farther away from the railroad station. They shared their new residence with several other Jews. It was crowded and lacked furniture, presumably looted by Germans or locals. Food remained scare, and the Silberfarbs wandered the streets and nearby forest looking for whatever scraps they could find. Such endeavors were often interrupted by bombings, forcing the family to run inside the nearest building for cover.

One day, Miashke tore through the home in panic. She had been given thirty minutes to pack and make it to the railroad station, where the Soviets would relocate her for work duty.

"Did they ask you your name?" Lea questioned her sister.

"No," Miashke responded.

"Then you're not going," Lea stated matter-of-factly.

Miashke explained that the Soviet soldiers were selecting able-bodied adults off the street to help with their military efforts. "But what will I do if they find out and come and get me?"

Lea shook her head. "They're not going to come and find you. They don't know who you are. And you're going to have a job."

Lea found Miashke a job as a seamstress for a wealthy family. The work gave Miashke protection from the Soviet soldiers and a few extra coins for food.

While living in Rafalivka, Sophia fell ill with typhus. An outbreak was sweeping the civilian populations and Allied Forces in Europe, buoyed by cramped and unclean conditions. Faced with no improvement and a climbing fever in her daughter, Lea carried Sophia to a local military hospital, begging the Soviets to treat her. They agreed on the condition that Lea work in the hospital as recompense. Lea spent day and night in the hospital, visiting Sophia, cleaning, and emptying bedpans for wounded soldiers. During breaks, she walked home to check on Bernie and Paula, sneaking out a piece of bread for them when she could.

A few days later, Paula woke up nauseated and feverish. She begged Bernie to fetch her some water, explaining that he had to boil it first for safety. Bernie found an empty coffee can, trekked to the nearest river to fill it, and boiled the water for Paula. By the time he returned, Paula had significantly deteriorated and was too weak to drink. She slept through the night, awakened the next morning by Lea carrying her to the hospital. As Paula and Sophia started to recover, Bernie began exhibiting typhus symptoms and quickly joined them in the hospital. Eventually, they all recuperated.

In July 1944, Soviet forces liberated Pinsk. Slightly northwest of Serniki, Pinsk was familiar to Lea and, as the nearest city, the likely site of return for any surviving Serniki Jews. Standing on the side of the road, Lea flagged down a Soviet Army truck and asked for a lift to Pinsk. The driver agreed, and Lea, her children, and Miashke piled into the back of the truck, sitting atop the barrels of kerosene that filled the truck bed. The ride was bumpy and uncomfortable with the metal digging into their skin, but the children were thrilled that for once they did not have to walk.

When they arrived in Pinsk, the Silberfarbs found few survivors from Serniki. No other relatives had escaped the ghetto, and most friends had perished either by Nazi gunfire or illness. Indeed, not long after meeting the Silberfarbs in Vychivka, Matis Bubrov died of tuberculosis.[1]

Lea spotted a home a block away from the marketplace. The Silberfarbs took one of the two bedrooms in the house, the other occupied by another Jewish family. The kitchen served as communal space for the two families, but it was dominated by Lea. She made cakes and rolls and breads, filling the home with the once-familiar scent of her baked goods and selling them in the market to afford more nutritious meals for her children.

The operation was not without risk. Running a business was still illegal under Soviet rule, and Lea was constantly looking over her shoulder to make sure that Soviet officials were not tailing her. On multiple occasions the NKVD brought her in at night for questioning, but they never could catch Lea in the act.

Living in Pinsk was still the closest to a normal life that the Silberfarbs had experienced in years. The city was fully liberated, and without the threat of constant bombings, they were removed from the ongoing war. The children enrolled in school, and Paula began the third grade as she was supposed to have done before the Nazis invaded. When the children fell ill, Lea could call a medical doctor for care and access real medications. Whether her children cooperated, however, was a separate question; Bernie was so terrified of doctors that when one made a house call in response to his complaints of a stomach ache, the boy jumped out the window to escape.

One morning, Lea was selling goods in the marketplace when she sensed that she was being watched. Worried that the Soviets had come to bust her operation, Lea began scanning the crowd around her. She noticed a man on the other side of the street, frozen in place and fixated on her. The pair locked eyes, both straining to determine whether the apparently familiar face was actually whom they thought. After a moment, Lea and Dimitro Lacunyetz were barreling toward each other. The two embraced. Through tears, Dimitro whispered into Lea's ear, "Now I can die in peace."

Dimitro had spent the prior two years worrying whether Lea and the children had survived in the forest. Lea, overcome with gratitude for the man who had helped keep her and her children alive when the Nazis had first invaded, offered Dimitro some baked goods, and the only possession of value she still had: her wedding band, which she kept covered by a rag wrapped around her finger to prevent it from being stolen during the war.

16

Conscripted into the Red Army, David was assigned a unit and uniform. The Red Army lacked the trucks needed to transport soldiers to the front, so it forced the new recruits to march across Poland. For months, David and his unit spent each day marching, lugging equipment, munitions, and food along the way. David, at twenty-two, was pushed to his breaking point as officers on horseback rode past the men shouting orders to speed up.

Every hour, the soldiers were given a brief respite. At the end of the five-minute break, David was so exhausted that he struggled to stand himself back up and resume the trek. By sunset, having traversed about fifty kilometers, David's legs were too fatigued to support his weight; he often resorted to crawling the last hundred meters on all fours until he reached the campsite for the night.

Though toughened from his days in the partisans, David was nonetheless taken aback by the Soviets' far from honorable behavior. The soldiers pillaged cities, forcing their way into homes where they slept and seized anything of value. Upon entering a new location, the Red Army killed with abandon, opening fire before even determining whether they were shooting an enemy or innocent civilian. Soviet soldiers raped thousands of girls and women, including German civilians and the Jews they liberated.[1]

Eventually, David made it to the Eastern Front. David's unit was a standby team. Until they were needed in direct combat, the recruits were assigned to various other support roles. David, after a short period of training, was tasked with maintaining the communication lines to the front. The Soviets were reluctant to use wireless communication, thinking cable lines were less likely to be compromised.[2] They were therefore reliant on a several-hundred-mile network of cable wires stretching all the way to the battlefield, which the soldiers hand laid and the enemy frequently cut.[3]

David ran around with a large spool of wire on his back, laying down new lines of communication as the Eastern Front continued to advance toward Germany. Artillery fire pummeled the area, leaving the wires in a constant state of disrepair. Fixing them was a dangerous task. David had to climb out of the trench and, while exposed to Nazi fire, replace the destroyed section of cable by splicing together the disconnected ends. The missions were completed late at night when movements were better masked, but the Nazis still managed to kill many of the Soviet cable technicians.

In late 1944, the Soviet-German front lined the two sides of the Bug River, a major waterway connecting the Baltic Sea with much of Poland. Soviet officers ordered David's unit into the trenches, telling the men that they would be conducting a training exercise. David climbed into the ditch, sandwiched between his comrades. To his left were two Soviet soldiers, tasked with operating machine guns that sat atop the trench edge. The area beyond the two men was unstaffed, as the earth sloped downward leaving too shallow a hole for protection. To David's right was a man named Gashinski, a fast friend and fellow Jewish conscript from Kiev. The remainder of the unit was lined up to the right of Gashinski.

It quickly became evident that their assignment to the trench was not a drill. Artillery began flying overhead, and the hazy air, shaking earth, and deafening explosions were disorienting. David stayed crouched against the ground, not daring to move and praying for the onslaught to stop; lifting a limb or head above the trench wall meant near-certain injury.

Even after the offensive ended, the night remained miserable.

The rain fell so hard that visibility was nearly impossible, and the trench devolved into a muddy mess. David's long army coat, soaked with muck and water, felt like it weighed a ton. He tried to keep his feet from soaking in the expanding puddles, fearing trench foot might set in.

Unbeknownst to the unit, two Germans paddled across the Bug River by boat from the German territory to the Soviet side. They traveled upstream of the machine-gun equipped soldiers, concealed by the dark, rainy conditions. When they reached the shore, the German soldiers traversed the unmanned lower area to the left of the trench and crawled around to the backside of the Soviet trench. Suddenly David heard gunshots behind him. He jumped up, turned around, and saw the two Nazi soldiers. "Germans!" David screamed.

Gashinski began running through the trench in the opposite direction. "David, run!" he shouted.

David, frozen in shock, snapped into reality and followed him. Looking back as he ran, David realized that nobody was running behind him.

The fleeing Red Army unit was halted by their captain. With a finger pointed back from where they had come, he commanded the unit to turn around. "Марш вперёд!" he shouted in Russian. David, the last in the line, suddenly became the leader. In front of him he could see the two Germans tying up their hostages, the two Soviet soldiers standing beside David earlier that night manning the machine guns.

David reached for his rifle but realized that in his hurry he had left it sitting atop the trench. He had few options. Walking forward meant that he would be attacked by the Germans; turning around would be met with the barrel of his commander's gun. Unwilling to die, David resorted to the only weapon he had. He pulled a hand grenade off his belt and heaved it at the two Germans.

The grenade exploded, killing the Nazi soldiers. The two Soviet hostages survived, albeit with serious injuries. One lost a leg. David was terrified, convinced that he would be killed by the Soviets for knowingly injuring his fellow soldiers.

After a sleepless night, David reported to roll call the following morning with his unit. The general commanded him to step forward. Realizing that his concerns of being reprimanded were materializing, David obeyed the order, his legs wobbling and his face growing hot with fear. When he reached the general, David took a deep breath, bracing himself for what would come.

Then the man started speaking. "We have somebody here today who is a hero," the general exclaimed. "David knew what he was doing. He understood that our soldiers would have been taken captive and killed after being forced to reveal compromising information. Instead, David saved them."

David stood dumbfounded as the general presented him with a medal.

"What would you like as a reward?" the general asked.

Unsure of what an appropriate response would be, David expressed his only real desire: "I want to see my father."

To David's astonishment, the general agreed.

As a prize for his heroism, David received about a month of furlough from the Red Army. He traveled to Lida by train, returning to the town where he had left his family the prior summer. When he arrived, Berko and Batya greeted him jubilantly, relieved to see him alive. Berko had been worried sick about his son, following news about the perilous battles taking place on the Eastern Front.

David was equally thrilled to find his family living relatively safe and well as liberated civilians. Berko had taken up work in a factory and was once again able to provide food for himself and his daughter. Rid of the Germans and devastated by warfare, the still-standing homes in Lida—mostly belonging to murdered Jews—became a free-for-all amongst the survivors. Berko, Batya, and Fishel had managed to claim a home for themselves, and Berko had somehow arranged for the Baran family to join them.

Esther Baran was the distant relative of Berko's wife for whom Berko had sent a food delivery in the Krasne ghetto. The Barans had lived in Gorodok, Poland, about eighty kilometers northeast of Iwje, until their eldest child, Moshe, was transported by the Germans to Krasne to build railroad tracks connecting Nazi warehouses to the Eastern Front.[4] Eventually the entire Baran family ended up in the Krasne ghetto, from which Moshe had managed to escape to the partisans.[5]

Moshe had organized the rescue of his mother, Esther, sister, Mina, and brother, Joshua.[6] His father and another sister had been killed in the liquidation of the Krasne ghetto—shot, jammed into a barn with countless others, and repeatedly set on fire until the heaps of bodies disintegrated to ash—before Moshe could finalize plans for their escape.[7] Between staying with a farmer and in a Jewish camp near the partisans, Esther, Joshua, and Mina had survived[8] and, with Berko's aid, made their way to join him in Lida. Moshe, who had remained active in the partisans during the war, was conscripted into the Red Army like David.[9]

Shortly after his arrival, David went for a walk with Batya. She wrapped her arms around his arm. "This lady came in here, and she wants to take the place of my mother," she said, teeming with resentment. "I am not going to let her do that."

David realized that Batya was referencing Esther Baran. While Esther and Berko maintained separate bedrooms, the implication was clear. David paused for a moment. "Batya, let me give you some advice," he said warmly. "Life has to go on. You cannot bring mom back, so don't take away from dad the privilege of enjoying what is left of his life."

Batya was stubborn, but the conversation did seem to temper some of her anger.

David was also stubborn. He was adamant about returning to Iwje. The Bakszts had heard rumors that nothing was left, but David wanted to see the remnants for himself. Berko tried to persuade David to leave the ugly past behind. "There's nothing there for us in Iwje. No Jews are left, nothing," Berko explained. But David was undeterred. Still donning his Red Army uniform, David flagged down horses and buggies on the main roadway in Lida until finding one bound for Iwje. "We're going with you," he demanded.

Berko and Batya, not wanting to leave David to travel alone, climbed into the wagon. After a couple of hours, they made the thirty-kilometer trip to Iwje. When they arrived at their childhood home, the Bakszts found it inhabited by non-Jewish Poles. The house looked the same, but more sterile. The *mezuzah* had been removed from the doorframe. Berko once again pleaded with David to give up on the visit. David knocked on the door.

When the new owner answered, David insisted that they be let inside. Powerless to question the command of a Soviet soldier, the resident acquiesced and the Bakszts entered their former home. What David found was both deeply familiar and entirely foreign. He recognized the couch and table in the living area on the right. David stepped farther inside and pushed open the door to his parents' old bedroom. Confronted with the bed where his mother used to sleep, David was overwhelmed. Suddenly, everything in the house was a visceral reminder of his mother. David ran out from the house, hysterically crying. Berko and Batya, upset themselves, tried to comfort David as he broke down in the front yard.

17

Eventually, it came time for David to return to the Red Army. Berko, uneasy at the prospect of him returning to war, insisted that David write to him. They devised a scheme so that David could discreetly communicate his whereabouts to Berko. David would form an acrostic that spelled out his location using the first letter of each line in the opening paragraph of his writings. Berko also demanded that David take some provisions along for the trip. He gave David whatever packaged food he could find in Lida, some bullions and canned meats left behind by the fleeing German Army and an empty can for water. David kissed Batya and Berko goodbye, and with no more than his rucksack, headed to the front.

When David arrived back at the Bug River in early 1945 he recognized no one. He had been left behind by his unit, met instead with a different Red Army regiment that knew nothing about him. David explained to an officer that he was looking for his unit after returning from furlough to visit his father in Lida. The officer took David inside a military outpost and searched his rucksack. "You came from Lida? What languages do you speak?" he asked.

David responded that he spoke Yiddish, Russian and Polish. The officer, unsatisfied, continued to ask David a series of questions. Another man entered the room with a large rifle. The armed officer situated himself in the corner, standing motionless with his eyes fixated on David.

The first officer exited the room. "You stand here, you can't leave."

David stayed put for hours. As night set in, a man from the NKVD entered the room. The secret police hounded David with even more questions. "Where did you get this German food? How did you get here?"

David reiterated his story, explaining that his father in Lida had given him the food and offering up his furlough papers as evidence.

The agents did not believe David. His rucksack filled with German goods and unexpected arrival led the Soviets to suspect that he was a spy. After a week of unrelenting questioning and constant supervision, David feared that he would ultimately be executed for espionage. But an officer finally returned and announced that David's story had been verified. "Would you like to join us or go to a different regiment?" they asked him. Unaware of his prior unit's whereabouts and not wanting to risk another identity mishap, David figured that he was best staying put.

In the new unit, David was again tasked with managing the communication infrastructure. Germany was rapidly losing territory. The Allies were at Germany's doorstep, separated only by the Rhine River in the west, and the Red Army was advancing through the Baltics toward Berlin.

David's unit was hurriedly relocated to Danzig, a port city located on the Baltic Coast. Home to many German nationals, Danzig had been part of Germany from the early 1800s until the end of the Great War, when it was declared a free city operating under the protections of the League of Nations.[1] Administratively tied to Poland, the city served as a crucial connection between the Baltic Sea and Poland.[2] Hitler was determined to regain control of Danzig and attacked the city in his initial invasion of Poland.[3] He quickly annexed Danzig, setting up the Stutthof Camp nearby, an internment camp that was converted into a labor camp and ultimately a concentration camp.[4]

In March 1945, Danzig was the site of a brutal battle between

German and Soviet forces. The Germans took aim at the Red Army from ships in the Baltic, bombarding the shore with gunfire. The explosions set off by the Germans were so violent that they blew several-meter-sized holes in the ground, spraying dirt and rocks into the air. David and two comrades took shelter inside a hole situated behind one of the many large trees that populated Danzig. As shelling poured down around them, one struck the ground just behind them. The explosion knocked David unconscious.

When he eventually came to, the firing had stopped. David woke to find himself sandwiched between the two lifeless bodies of his fellow soldiers. He was disoriented, his thinking clouded by a piercing blare and his vision hazy from the dusty air. As he struggled to sit himself up, David realized that the entire right side of his face was paralyzed; his mouth drooped downward, his right eye was stuck shut, and but for the indelible ringing, his ear detected no sound. He tried to speak. Nothing came out.

Still in shock the next day, David was sent to a military doctor. He tried to explain to the doctor what had occurred, but David could not verbalize more than a few stuttered syllables. The doctor told him that there was a chance the paralysis would wear off, but it was impossible to predict how long, if ever, it would take until he began to see improvement. David's frustration was palpable. "You are young," the doctor said, encouragingly. "Eat."

Determined to regain his speech, David took the advice to heart. He wandered into a local barn and grabbed a pail full of raw eggs. David sat down with the bucket in his lap and used a needle to punch a small hole in an egg. He pressed the egg against his puckered lips, sucked out the raw insides, and moved on to the next egg. By the end of the day, David had eaten the entire bucketful.

During the ordeal, David corresponded with his father by mail. He received a letter back from Berko stating that Berko and Batya had decided to relocate from Lida to Lodz, another Polish city closer to Germany and almost due south of Danzig. They had heard that Jewish refugees were being discreetly routed from Lodz through Greece into Palestine by a Zionist organization called the *Bericha*. They thought it was their best hope to make it to the Holy

Land, the only place that they knew of where the Jewish community continued to thrive.

Over the next few weeks, David slowly regained control over the right side of his face. His eye reopened, his ears stopped buzzing, and the paralysis wore off. Eventually, the hearing fully returned to his right ear. Once recuperated, David was immediately transferred to the new Eastern Front, this time within Germany's borders. The Red Army and German forces were battling it out on opposite sides of the Elbe River, exchanging continuous fire as the Germans tried to hold off the Soviets' advance into the country.

The Elbe River was wide, and though the Soviets could not fully traverse it, they managed to gain a foothold on an island situated midway. But the soldiers on the island had no means to communicate with the main unit on the eastern shoreline. Still committed to only using wired communications, the Red Army needed someone to run a cable from the coast to the island.

The task was the functional equivalent of a death sentence. A constant stream of bullets skimmed the surface of the water, striking anyone who attempted to travel across the river. One by one, nine soldiers from David's unit were assigned the mission of connecting the island to the Soviet communication network, and one by one each soldier was shot before reaching the landmass. David's lieutenant was fond of him and tried to avoid sending David. But eventually the lieutenant ran out of alternative options.

David waited until nightfall. He took a small wooden rowboat and rigged up a spool of wire so that it would automatically unravel out the back of the boat as it moved forward. David then pointed the bow in the direction of the island and climbed inside. He lay down flat on his stomach, tightly pressing his torso against the bottom of the boat. With his arms outstretched and resting against the edges of the boat, David used his hands to paddle, moving nothing but his wrists. As the boat slowly moved across the water, David heard the bullets whizzing above his body. He kept his head down and continued to paddle, unsure whether he was even still headed in the right direction. David was quietly praying for a miracle.

David made it to the island. After successfully setting up communications for the soldiers, he was faced with the decision of whether or not to stay put. The trip back to the Soviet camp was dangerous, but staying on the island left him vulnerable to the barrage of German air strikes that would inevitably resume pelting the island come daybreak. David decided it was best to head back to the shore while he could.

He climbed back into the boat and began paddling. David was all alone on the river, with nothing but the sound of bullets to keep him company. His hands grew tired from paddling and his body sore from the unforgiving bottom of the boat. Unable to lift his head, David struggled to direct the boat in the right direction.

David finally felt the thump of the boat hitting land. To his and his lieutenant's shock, he completed the mission and made it back alive to the Soviet side of the Elbe. Once safely in the trenches, David took off his overcoat. Running down the back of the coat were long pleats that stuck out slightly from his body. Passing cleanly through the pleated fabric were bullet holes.

18

On an evening in April 1945, David marched into Magdeburg, Germany. The soldiers found the city decimated from a British air raid undertaken in mid-January. Knowing the end of the war was imminent, they decided that a celebration was in order. The Soviet soldiers—fueled by copious amounts of vodka—spent the night dancing and shouting in the streets. Dawn greeted them drunken and bleary eyed.

Suddenly, shooting erupted from all directions. Glass was flying as German soldiers fired out of windows and basements. David, in better cognitive form than most of his comrades, managed to duck into a nearby home. He climbed inside a cellar and stayed hidden for hours, listening for the sounds of artillery fire to dissipate. Catching them off-guard and off-balance, the Germans inflicted a short-lived but devastating blow to the Red Army. Nearly all the Soviet soldiers in the city were killed.

Over the next few days, the Soviet Army, fortified with new arrivals, leveled Magdeburg. As David slogged through the rubble-ridden streets, he suddenly saw lines of tanks in the distance, pouring into the city. Panicked that they were once again under attack by the Germans, David picked up the radio he was tasked with carrying as a communications officer. "The Germans are coming in with tanks! We need an air raid! Now!" he screamed frantically.

The officer on the other side responded sternly, "Don't do anything. Don't shoot. These are our allies!"

David could not believe his ears.

In mid-April 1945, American troops entered Magdeburg as the Eastern and Western Fronts converged. The two armies spoke different languages, but their shared glee was unmistakable. The American and Soviet soldiers hugged and kissed each other as tears streamed down their faces. Exchanging whatever they had, the Soviet soldiers gifted vodka, and the Americans offered cigarettes and chocolate. The allies spent the day celebrating in the streets, realizing that the long-awaited end had finally arrived. Shortly thereafter, the Germans surrendered.

As joyous as the site was, it was also harrowing. Jews walked by foot out of the recently liberated extermination camps, emaciated and wandering hundreds of kilometers back to hometowns and families that no longer existed. David approached a group of Jewish women on the side of a roadway, and they immediately cowered in fear. He realized that the women, seeing a blonde, fair-skinned man in a Soviet uniform, were concerned that he might rape them. David tried to quell their fears by speaking in Yiddish, "Don't be afraid. I'm Jewish." The women relaxed slightly, and David insisted that they take whatever food he had. He asked them to look up his father if they passed through Lodz and let him know that David was okay.

David was unsure where the Soviet Army would send him now that Germany had fallen. Nervous that he would be shipped off to the Motherland or another battle site, David asked for a few days furlough to visit his father, who he claimed still lived in Lida. His commander approved the request.

The trains from Germany to Poland were packed with survivors attempting to reunite with family members. David could not even find available standing area. Determined to get out of Germany and away from the Red Army as quickly as possible, David climbed up the side of a full train bound east through Lodz. When he pulled himself onto the roof of one of the cars, David saw that several other men had had the same idea.

The ride to Lodz was lengthy—600 kilometers—and restless. David not only had to hold onto the roof of the speeding train but also keep an eye out for tunnels. Whenever the train approached an underpass, David would carefully lay himself flat against the roof of the train to fit within the tunnel's clearance.

The train eventually reached Lodz, stopping for about an hour before moving onward along its route. David waited several minutes, not wanting to attract attention as a stowaway or a member of the Red Army, before climbing down from the roof. When he reached the street level, David pulled out the folded-up letter from his father containing the Bakszts' address in Lodz. He approached a few people on the street asking directions, and they pointed him to a trolley. After a ride on the streetcar and a brief walk, David knocked on the door of his father's home.

Berko immediately pulled David inside the house and closed the door. He kissed and hugged his son tightly, neither of the pair believing that David had made it back unscathed. Berko demanded that David remove the Soviet uniform straightaway and handed his son a set of his own civilian clothes. Berko's pants were roughly three times David's size, and the young man was swimming in the fabric held up only by a tightly pulled belt. Before David was fully dressed, Berko snatched the Soviet uniform and carried it over to the front window. He removed a piece of wood that sat below the windowsill, revealing a gap between the interior and exterior walls of the home. Berko stuffed the Soviet uniform as deep as he could inside the hole and sealed the space back up immediately.

The reunited family disagreed on where to go next, but nobody wanted to stay in Poland. Batya and Fishel were adamant about moving to Palestine, longing to live among a growing Jewish community where they would no longer be worried about persecution. Berko and David believed the United States offered a more promising start than a burgeoning country, and Berko's two brothers, Isaac and Willie, were already well established in New York.

A team from the United Nations Relief and Rehabilitation Administration (UNRRA) set up a registration center in Lodz. The UNRRA established displaced persons camps across Germany, Austria, and Italy to provide basic food, shelter, and medical care for refugees until arrangements could be made for repatriation or immigration.[1] The camps varied tremendously in quality,[2] occupying abandoned warehouses, former concentration camps, and military barracks.[3]

With no means of immigrating anywhere in the short term, Berko, his children, and Fishel registered with the UNRRA. They were assigned to a camp in Austria and soon found themselves traversing Eastern Europe aboard a series of trains and buses. With a group of Jewish refugees, they passed through Poland, Czechoslovakia, and Austria before landing at a displaced persons camp on the Austria-Germany border in November 1945.

19

On May 5, 1945, the Silberfarbs stirred from sleep to find their house shaking. The windows rattled as people banged on building facades and danced in the streets. As the Silberfarbs regained consciousness, the muffled shouting became increasingly discernible. "The war is over! The war is over!" echoed through the city of Pinsk.

Over the following days, information and rumors swelled. Refugees and Allied fighters began surfacing in the city, including Miashke's husband, with stories about the atrocities they had witnessed. Soviet officials explained to the surviving Jews that anyone who had held Polish citizenship before the war was entitled to travel to any major city where they could journey onward to Palestine.

The Silberfarbs were tempted. They were too afraid to return to Serniki, paranoid that the new owners of their home and possessions may try to kill them to keep them from reclaiming their property. The idea of being surrounded by other Jews in Palestine was more appealing than rebuilding in a country that had demonstrated its utter disdain for the Jewish people. The family boarded a train for a lengthy ride across Poland to Lodz, where a Jewish agency was believed to be transporting Jews to Palestine.

In actuality, Jewish immigration to Palestine was severely restricted. The region—which the League of Nations had placed under British control in the aftermath of World War I to "secure the establishment of the Jewish national home" and safeguard "the civil and religious rights of all the inhabitants of Palestine, irrespective of race and religion"[1]—devolved into conflict as Zionists, Arabs, and British authorities clashed over its division. Notwithstanding hostilities, the Jews in Palestine experienced significant immigration and economic growth in the interwar period.[2]

But just as other countries had closed their doors to Jewish refugees fleeing Nazi Germany, British authorities backtracked from their promise of a Jewish homeland, and, in 1939, instituted new restrictions on Jewish immigration to Palestine.[3] Thousands of undocumented Jews attempted to enter Palestine by boat, many drowning in the process.[4] The practice only increased in the post-war period, with British forces apprehending and detaining the vast majority of Jewish refugees seeking to smuggle their way in.[5]

Upon reaching Lodz, the Silberfarbs were informed that they could not travel directly to Palestine but first had to transfer to a displaced persons camp. The camp assignment process was opaque. Jews were sent to various locales across the continent with assurances that the relocation would advance immigration to their favored destination. Miashke and Chaim were sent to Italy. The next day, Lea, Bernie, Paula, and Sophia were bound for Austria. The ride was lengthy, though exciting for the children who had never been on a commercial train. While they looked out the windows in astonishment, the views were more harrowing for Lea; streets in Budapest and Vienna were reduced to piles of rubble.

In October 1945, the Silberfarbs reached Ranshofen, a displaced persons camp on the Austria-Germany border in the American zone. Ranshofen was located just outside Braunau am Inn, Adolf Hitler's birthplace, and consisted of a collection of repurposed military barracks that housed approximately 250 Jews. Conditions at the camp were relatively good. Lea and her children were assigned to a four-apartment brick building and, for the first time in their lives, had running water and a proper oven. The Silberfarbs' apartment was shared with two other families, and consisted of two small bedrooms, one large bedroom, a living room, a kitchen, and a bathroom. The UNRRA supplied clothing and canned food that Lea bartered for butter and fresh vegetables.

Not long after the Silberfarbs had arrived, a large family living in the apartment vacated to travel onward, leaving just the Silberfarbs and one other family. Lea and the children moved into the large bedroom, freeing up the smaller room and the shared living room that had been functioning as an additional bedroom. The second small bedroom was populated by a couple, newly pregnant. Then a third family arrived, refilling the empty third bedroom.

As soon as he entered his new apartment, David Bakszt noticed the elder Silberfarb daughter. She looks pretty from behind, David thought to himself, fixated on her shiny dark hair pulled back loosely in a ribbon. When Paula turned around to introduce herself to the new residents, David noticed that she was rather attractive from the front too.

Despite being nine years apart in age, David and Paula quickly developed a kinship. They bonded over their common experiences during the war and spent evenings walking around the camp together. One night, David asked Paula if she would like to go out with him. She agreed, and David walked her to a small nearby restaurant for a drink. David ordered beer, Paula a lemonade.

The displaced persons camp provided a decent life for the relatively few children who had survived. The camp set up a makeshift school, where adults taught the Jewish children basic Hebrew, math, and history. It also had a Zionist youth group, a camp choir in which Sophia Silberfarb starred, and intramural sports teams. Paula and David spent most of their time together, but they too picked up hobbies. Paula practiced arithmetic and took a sewing class. David played on a volleyball team. But even in their Jewish bubble, remnants of antisemitism still crept in. Protestors gathered in Braunau, demanding that the Jewish refugees be removed from Ranshofen and demolishing the local synagogue.[6]

David and Paula were not the only ones with an escalating relationship. By early 1946, Fishel—who was living in another apartment in Ranshofen—and Batya were discussing marriage. Berko was opposed to the union, convinced that Fishel would never outgrow his rough-and-tumble background. He tried to keep Batya inside the apartment and away from Fishel, but it was useless. On March 14, 1946, the couple snuck away from the displaced persons camp to wed. Berko, having discovered the plan, chased after Batya and showed up at the ceremony. But unable to actually prevent the union and sympathetic to his daughter's pleas that he not spoil her wedding day, Berko did not object and instructed the couple to return to Ranshofen afterwards. A few months later, Batya was pregnant.

That spring, the Baran family arrived in Austria. They and the Bakszts had separated in Poland, when Berko, Batya, and Fishel had relocated to Lodz, and Esther, Mina, and Joshua had arranged to reunite with Moshe. Eventually, the Baran family also made their way to Lodz and were sent to Camp Wegscheid in Linz, Austria.[7] Camp Wegscheid was not too far from Ranshofen, and Berko occasionally visited Esther and a few other Iwje survivors housed at another nearby camp, Bindermichel.

Unlike the livable apartments in Ranshofen, conditions at Camp Wegscheid were deplorable. Garbage littered the grounds, plumbing often backed up, and sewage overflowed from cesspits.[8] No cultural or vocational training was available, and from their huts, Jews could hear the antisemitic chants of German collaborators sheltered at a neighboring camp.[9] Wegscheid was appropriately dubbed by American authorities as one of the worst camps in the American zone of Austria.[10] Berko suggested that the Barans come join them in Ranshofen instead, and the Barans agreed.

The Silberfarb, Bakszt, and Baran families grew close to one another, sharing meals and free time together. Moshe and David developed a particular kinship having had such similar experiences during the war, though Moshe played second fiddle to Paula. David and Paula became inseparable, a source of both great respite and stress for them as the possibility of their families immigrating to different countries grew increasingly likely.

Given antisemitic immigration quotas in Western nations and continued restrictions on Jewish settlement in Palestine,[11] many Jews in displaced persons camps saw only two options: sneak into Palestine or try to seek entry in countries where extended families could provide sponsorship. David and Berko were still determined to relocate to the United States, while Batya and Fishel were preparing to smuggle their way into Palestine. Lea, meanwhile, was deciding between Palestine and Cuba, having exchanged letters with Samuel's family in Havana who offered to take them in.

Even with familial sponsorship, obtaining a visa to immigrate was met with bureaucracy and opacity. Certain displaced persons camps provided better access to certain countries, and families often traveled between different camps depending on their preferred final destination. Germany-based camps were alleged to be a better stepping stone to America, and Italy to Palestine.

In late 1946, Berko decided that he and David should make their way to a camp in Hofgeismar, Germany. David said goodbye to his teary-eyed girlfriend, promising Paula that if she could convince her mother to move to Havana instead of Israel, David would be close enough in America to come and find her at her uncle's home.

By early 1947, Fishel and Batya had left Austria for Italy. Lea, meanwhile, was still uncertain of where to go. She and her children remained at Ranshofen for a total of two years, until the camp closed in 1948 and the Silberfarbs and Barans were both relocated to another displaced persons camp farther east in Ebelsberg, Austria.

Bernie and Sophia were adamant about immigrating to Palestine. Paula stayed silent, hoping that they would join their family in Cuba so she could be closer to David but thinking it unfair to let her romantic interests influence such a major family decision. Lea wrote to Bushe—Samuel's sister—and Bushe's husband Nucham, explaining that she felt compelled to honor

Bernie and Sophia's wishes. Several weeks later, she received a handwritten letter in the mail from Nucham:

> I understand that after what you've lived through, you want to be in a Jewish country. But many refugees are traveling to Palestine, and the Jewish agencies cannot tend to everybody. You will still be alone there. If you come to us, we'll help you raise your children. Give it a year, and if after a year you decide that you do not like living in Cuba, we will send you to Israel as immigrants, not as refugees.

Faced with no legitimate means of entry into Palestine and an exceedingly generous offer from Nucham to sponsor Lea and her children's move to Cuba, Lea acquiesced.

The displaced persons camp in Hofgeismar was built from repurposed German barracks. About thirty kilometers north of the German city of Kassel, it was controlled by the Americans and run by its residents as a small town.[12] With nearly 2,000 inhabitants, Hofgeismar's displaced persons camp was overcrowded, and two or three families shared a single room.[13] But the camp still afforded a decent quality of life with a Tarbut school, sports teams, and a hospital.[14] World ORT, a Jewish vocational training agency, also established a school to train residents in skills such as tailoring, radio technology, electrical engineering, and mechanics.[15]

Applying for a United States visa was a protracted process. David and Berko required a sponsor in the United States—Berko's brother Willie—and had to submit copious paperwork. Complicating matters was that Berko and David lacked identifying documentation due to the war. Eventually, they were offered an immigration interview. Berko had heard from other Jews in Hofgeismar that the Americans were prioritizing entry of concentration camp survivors. Hoping to help their chances at securing a coveted immigration spot, Berko told the officer conducting their interview that he and David had been in a concentration camp.

"Which camp?" the officer asked.

"Auschwitz," Berko immediately replied.

The officer grabbed Berko's left arm and turned it over. "Where is your number?" All Jewish prisoners were tattooed with an identification number upon arrival at Auschwitz. Berko's left forearm was conspicuously bare, and the officer knew he was lying. "Okay then, when you walk into Auschwitz, which side is the kitchen on?" the officer asked.

Berko took a guess, hoping the fifty-fifty shot might pay off. He guessed wrong.

Shortly thereafter, David and Berko's visas were denied, and their cases were closed.

PHOTOS

Left to right: David Bakszt, Batya Bakszt, Fishel Bialobroda, during David's furlough from the Soviet Army. Lida, Poland, January 3, 1945.

Batya Bakszt on a UNRRA truck. Location and date unknown.

Left to right: Fishel Bialobroda, Batya Bakszt, Berko Bakszt, David Bakszt. Ranshofen, Austria, date unknown.

Batya Bakszt and Fishel Bialobroda at their wedding in Austria, 1946.

Left to right: David Bakszt and Berko Bakszt. Ranshofen, Austria, 1946.

David Bakszt and Batya Bakszt in Ranshofen, Austria, date unknown.

Sophia Silberfarb, location and date unknown.

Left to right: Sophia Silberfarb and Paula Silberfarb, location and date unknown.

David Bakszt and Paula Silberfarb in Ranshofen, Austria, 1946.

David Bakszt and Paula Silberfarb in Ranshofen, Austria, 1946.

Left to right: Lea Silberfarb and her friend Bashke Fialkov. Ranshofen, Austria, 1946.

Miashke Koifman and Chaim Leib Koifman in a displaced persons camp in Italy, 1947.

20

After arriving in Italy, Batya and Fishel made contact with the *Haganah*, a Zionist paramilitary organization. Its enlisted defense force, the *Palmach*, smuggled Jewish refugees from Europe to Palestine during and after the war by ship.[1] The *Haapala* (undocumented immigrant) ships were dingy if not dangerous. They suffered frequent equipment failures and were often captured; of the sixty-five ships carrying 70,000 *Haapala* sent to Palestine between 1945 and 1948, only thirteen small ships with 2,500 Jews made it past the British authorities.[2] More than 2,000 people drowned or otherwise perished in transit.[3]

With the *Haganah*'s assistance, Batya and Fishel traveled to Sète, France, and boarded the *Theodor Herzl* on April 2, 1947, with 2,639 other Jewish passengers.[4] The filled-to-the-brim ship was inhospitable for an eight-months pregnant woman. Its lower deck was packed floor to ceiling with sleeping bunks, and many passengers fell ill to seasickness. The vessel, purchased from the Americans after being used during the war to lay telephone cable wires,[5] traveled the 2,000 nautical miles to Haifa on a malfunctioning coal engine that maxed out at eight knots.[6] Its frequent equipment failures panicked the passengers and forced the crew to reroute its course.[7] There were issues with the water supply aboard, the radios glitched, and the ventilation system failed.[8]

The risk that the British might capture the ship was also a constant concern. On night eight of the journey, as the ship neared Crete, Greece, two British reconnaissance aircrafts circled above. The aircrafts then disappeared into the night, apparently failing to identify the vessel as a *Haapala* ship in the darkness.[9] Another close call came the next day, when a patrolling destroyer warship shined its spotlight in the direction of the *Herzl*.[10] Assuming that the ship had been detected, its protective escorts began readying the Jews for confrontation, distributing defensive equipment—rubber sticks, gas masks, and brass knuckles—and setting up obstacles around the vessel.[11] The assault never came.[12]

Two days later, on the evening of April 13, 1947, the ship made its approach into Palestine's territorial waters near the Herzliya shoreline.[13] A British destroyer detected the unauthorized ship and began pursuing it.[14] The immigrants tried to lose the tail, raining bottles and other objects on the destroyer from the boat's stern.[15] The navigator's avoidance tactics coupled with choppy waters made seizure difficult for the British soldiers, and the *Herzl* held the British off for some time.[16] But armed with water hoses and tear gas, seven of the thirty-person British takeover crew eventually breached the vessel.[17]

When the British climbed aboard, the Jewish crowd surrounded the officials, preventing them from entering the navigation bridge.[18] Unable to free themselves and their tear-gas grenades depleted, the British soldiers allegedly grew fearful of the immigrants.[19] They pulled out their personal guns, which the soldiers were only authorized to use for self-defense purposes, and began firing into the air.[20] But after some of the soldiers mistakenly believed that the immigrants were returning fire, the British began shooting their weapons into the crowd of Holocaust survivors.[21]

Two hours later, fortified by the arrival of a second destroyer, the British subdued the Jewish resistance and seized control of the ship.[22] Ten immigrants were shot, with three young men dying from their wounds.[23] Twenty-three Jews were injured in the confrontation, sixteen seriously.[24]

Batya and Fishel were unharmed but trapped on an unstable boat being towed to an unknown location by the British authorities. On April 15, 1947, the ship docked at the Port of Haifa.[25] The Jewish passengers were held onboard until arrangements could be made for offloading and internment. As they waited, the passengers hung a long banner off the side of the ship: "The Germans destroyed our families & homes. Don't you destroy our hopes."[26] From the deck, Batya could finally see the land she longed for, stretching vastly before her eyes and entirely inaccessible.

The British officials disembarked the Jews in batches. The first day, about 1,500 Jews walked down the gangway, tired and defeated. They were shuffled through a disinfectant station, sprayed with DDT (now classified as a toxin and likely carcinogen), packed into four British corvettes, and sailed across the eastern Mediterranean Sea to Cyprus.[27] The remaining 1,200 Jews were held onboard the *Herzl* for multiple days due to a short supply of British deportation ships.[28]

Because Batya was visibly pregnant, the authorities offered her the option of staying in Palestine at the Atlit Detention Camp. Located just south of Haifa, it was where the sick and injured undocumented immigrants were kept. But the British refused to allow Fishel to accompany his wife, and Batya was unwilling to be separated from her husband. Batya and Fishel thus joined the overwhelming majority of *Herzl* passengers in Cyprus.

After over twelve hours of travel, the detainees made landfall in the southeast of Cyprus.[29] The Jews were loaded into a series of military trucks and driven past the beach and into an internment camp surrounded by barbed wire. British military authorities stood guard, sitting atop watchtowers armed with guns.[30] For many Jews, the view brought to the surface traumatic memories of concentration camps and ghetto walls;[31] they hung protest signs: "From Dachau to Cyprus."[32]

Camp 68 was one of twelve detention camps on the Island, situated within the cluster of camps 64 through 69 in

Xylotymbou.[33] It was empty when the *Herzl* passengers arrived, filled with canvas tents and a few tin communal structures in the center, all erected by the German prisoners of war held in another nearby camp.[34]

The Jewish detainees were packed into the tents and forced to live in conditions that rivaled the worst of Europe's displaced persons camps.[35] Baking in the hot desert sun, strangers shared limited tent space that lacked privacy, running water, and electricity.[36] There was no furniture other than beds, and food and clothing supplies were inadequate.[37] Without a sewer system, the Camp reeked.[38] By the time a second group of Jews were transported to Camp 68 a few days later, all tent space was fully allocated; the immigrants, passengers on the captured ship *Hatikva*, were forced to sleep on the bare ground.[39]

The Joint Distribution Committee (JDC), a Jewish humanitarian organization, did what it could to make life in the internment camps more bearable, despite resistance from the British.[40] It recruited medical teams from Palestine to provide basic health care, which was desperately needed as the unsanitary and cramped conditions fed outbreaks of skin diseases and infections.[41] The JDC worked to increase food supplies on the Island and provide basic education to the growing population of children. It also fostered opportunities for religious observance and skill development through vocational training and workshops.[42]

Over the two-and-a-half years that Jewish Holocaust survivors were interned in Cyprus, 2,000 babies were born in the Jewish wing of the British military hospital in Nicosia.[43] Included in that statistic is Rochelle, born to Batya and Fishel Bialobroda on May 26, 1947.

The Bialobroda family raised their daughter in the camp for the first six months of her life. As fall approached, the Western World was growing increasingly horrified with Britain's cruel and sometimes violent handling of the Holocaust survivors. But it also remained generally unwilling to absorb the population into its own borders. The United Nations began weighing proposals for a permanent partitioning of Palestine and the establishment of an official Jewish state.[44]

Seeing the writing on the wall, Zionist intelligence grew concerned about the Jews' preparedness to stave off an Arab attack upon a British withdrawal from the region.[45] The Cyprus Jews had come to the attention of Golda Meir, the future prime minister of Israel and then-leader of the political department of the Jewish Agency, which sought to facilitate Jewish settlement in Palestine and served as a Zionist liaison to the British.[46] Meir perceived the growing population of Jewish babies in Cyprus as a potential solution to the defense problem.[47] Allowing them and their parents to immigrate would both increase Jewish settlement in Palestine and broaden the population of young men capable of coming to a budding nation's defense.[48] It would also serve humanitarian purposes; there were growing concerns that the babies would not survive in the camps, where a typhus outbreak had taken hold.[49]

Each month, half of the 1,500-Jewish-immigration quota to Palestine was filled by Jews detained in Cyprus,[50] operating on a first-in, first-out system.[51] Meir persuaded the British authorities to move up the December Cyprus transport on the condition that the Jewish refugees agree to the prioritization of families with babies.[52]

On November 10, 1947, Meir visited the camps with the difficult task of persuading the refugees to consent to the arrangement.[53] She climbed atop a makeshift stage made of overturned vegetable crates and addressed the crowd of fellow Jews: "There is typhus here in the camps. We cannot allow Jewish babies to die. We owe them life. I am asking you to make a sacrifice, that some of you, who are slated to leave this month, give up your right and wait for next month."[54] Angry voices interrupted her, frustrated at all the sacrifices they had already made over the past decade in Europe.

"Friends, hear me," Meir continued.[55] "If we delay getting the little children right out, they may die. We want them to live. We want you to live. We want all of you to come home."[56] As Meir begged the crowd, one woman volunteered her certificate, explaining that her babies had already died.[57] Then another person stepped up. And another.

The appeal worked. On November 28, 1947, the "babies' ship" brought countless mothers, fathers, and infants to Palestine.[58] Aboard the ship were the Bialobrodas. They traveled to Tel Aviv, where Fishel's extended family took them in. The following day, the United Nations General Assembly endorsed a resolution to partition Palestine between the Jews and Arabs with Jerusalem falling under international administration.[59] Two days after the Bialobrodas had arrived, violence broke out.[60]

21

In Hofgeismar, David spent his time writing letters to Paula and Batya and reapplying for visas. He came up with the idea of submitting his and his father's visa applications anew, using their middle names in place of their forenames with the hope that the American authorities would not associate the applications with their previously rejected ones.

In May 1948, as the Bakszts were waiting to hear about the status of their visa applications, Berko decided to undergo treatment for his hernia. "I don't trust the German doctors here," David said, asking his father to delay the surgery. "There are better doctors in America." But Berko was insistent that he not come to America as a burden. He had plans to open a business in New York and wanted to arrive with the strength to do so immediately. Berko made a surgical appointment at a nearby hospital.

On the day of his procedure, Berko waited for David at the entryway to their building. David walked down the four flights of stairs from the apartment to the ground floor, his heart sinking deeper into his stomach with each step. "I don't want you to go," David said weepy as he reached his father. Berko gave his son a hug and kiss and departed for the hospital.

For the first few days after the surgery, it appeared to be a success. David was deeply relieved, spending most waking hours at the side of his father's hospital bed. Then suddenly, Berko took a turn for the worse. Over the course of several days, he grew weaker as his organs began to fail, likely the result of a postoperative infection. David remained at Berko's bedside, praying that his father recover and David be spared from enduring yet another devastating loss. On the eighth day after surgery, Berko told David to remember to take care of his sister. Shortly thereafter, on May 28, 1948, Berko died.

Suddenly David found himself completely alone in Germany. Though death had become a familiar presence in his life, the loss of his father was more than he could bear. Berko had become a father, mother, and companion to David, protecting the young man through the war and guiding him in its aftermath. Even as their lives returned to the realm of normalcy, Berko had assumed a caregiver role, managing the cooking and cleaning at the displaced persons camps.

David sunk into a deep depression. He barely slept, kept awake by his frantic brain. Multiple times each night, David climbed out of bed and sprinted down the stairs and around the camp, hoping in vain to outrun his nightmares.

Seeking comfort, David tried to write to Paula in Ebelsberg, but his letters went unanswered. Unbeknownst to him, she was already en route to Cuba. Occasionally David received letters from Batya, updating him about how much little Rochelle had grown and the status of the Arab-Israeli War. But David's responses slowed to a near halt; he was too devastated at the prospect of trying to put into words what had happened. Batya noticed her brother's waning correspondence and the conspicuous lack of responses to questions about how their father was doing. After several months of David dodging her questions, Batya sent a letter demanding an update on Berko. David wrote to his sister, explaining that Berko had died and was buried in a small Jewish cemetery on a hilltop in Hofgeismar, which he visited frequently.

Batya was distraught. She was particularly troubled by the absence of any place that she could visit to feel connected to her father. Batya could not leave her family to travel to the grave in Germany; Israel had descended into a war zone after five surrounding nations invaded the new country.

In June 1948, the Silberfarbs boarded a series of trains from Austria to France. As promised, Nucham coordinated for Lea and her children to immigrate to Cuba, covering the entire cost. He handled their visa applications and transportation arrangements, sending them all the necessary paperwork to board a Havana-bound ship in Paris. The Silberfarbs arrived at the dock at the scheduled time, but the ship never appeared.

Panicked, Lea called Nucham, who contacted HIAS, the Hebrew Immigrant Aid Society, which assisted Jewish refugees. HIAS informed Nucham that Cuba was imminently closing its borders to Jewish immigrants from Europe; the Silberfarbs had to enter the country immediately to be admitted. Waiting for another ship was not an option. With Nucham footing the hefty bill, HIAS arranged for the four Silberfarbs to board a propeller plane from Paris.

It was the first time any of the Silberfarb children had been on a plane, and the lengthy trip itself was an attraction. Paula peered out the window with amazement and trepidation as the small plane miraculously lifted itself off the ground and the vast continent shrunk into the distance.

When they landed in Havana many hours later, the Silberfarbs were greeted enthusiastically by Samuel's sisters and their families: Bushe and Nucham Rozen, with their children Simon and Sophie; and Mary and Solomon Milner, with their girls Elsa and Sophia. Though they had never spent much time with the Rozens and Milners and the relation extended from Samuel's lineage, Lea and her children were immediately treated as close family by their Cuban relatives. The Milners and Rozens had lost several family members during the war—Nucham's brother and mother and Bushe and Mary's brother and father—and appreciated the significance of having surviving relatives join them.

Nucham sought to make the Silberfarbs' transition to life in Cuba as seamless as possible. He moved his wife and children out of their three-bedroom apartment, located mere blocks from the ocean, so that Lea and her children could live there. The Silberfarbs found an apartment at 204 Merced Street waiting for them, fully furnished and stocked with food, bedding, and anything else they might need during their first few weeks in Cuba.

The Silberfarbs quickly grew close to the Rozens and Milners, in large part due to Nucham's persistent efforts to make them feel welcomed. When Nucham began taking driving lessons, he made a point to always stop by the Silberfarb apartment to see if Bernie, Paula, or Sophia wanted to tag along for a ride. The Rozen and Milner children befriended their Silberfarb cousins, all of whom were in a similar age range. Lea, still an observant Jew, even made an exception to the religious rule against operating a car on holidays so that the families could celebrate together.

Nucham owned a fabric store where he employed Paula and Bernie. For Bernie, the job was a mere stepping stone until he could branch out on his own and pursue aspirations of commanding a larger business. But Paula loved working in Nucham's store and took her responsibilities in earnest. Each morning she was the first to arrive, opening the doors and setting up before other employees and customers began trickling in. She spent all day diligently working in the store, using a ruler to precisely measure each piece of purchased fabric and even notifying Nucham when she suspected another employee was undercharging customers. Paula's presence was a tremendous help to Nucham, freeing up time for him and his wife outside the store.

One summer day, Paula's cousins were planning to go to the beach. Over Paula's objections, Nucham insisted that his niece enjoy a day off. Paula reluctantly agreed, leaving her Aunt Bushe to watch over the store. When Paula returned to the shop the next morning, Nucham asked her to count the money in the register from the prior day's transactions. Paula leafed through the bills, counting as she typically did, when she noticed that one looked odd. She plucked it out, inspected it, and turned to her uncle. "I hate to tell you this," Paula began, "but there's something wrong with this bill." Nucham already knew. Bushe had accidentally accepted a counterfeit bill, and Nucham wanted to see whether Paula would have caught it. She did and solidified his trust in her in the process.

In vivid detail, David watched his mother approach him. Her arm was outstretched, handing him an envelope. David took the envelope and drew it closer to his face to examine it. The front contained a round stamp marked "8 Dec." "You will be okay," Rochel said. David awoke from his dream, his less-pleasant reality coming back into focus but accompanied by a bit more optimism for a change.

A few days later there was a knock on the door of David's apartment. The postman handed David a single envelope. It contained a round stamp with a postmark date of December 8, 1948. Inside, David found a letter from the American consulate with his visa. He was abundantly lucky. Not only did David receive one of only 200,000 displaced persons visas offered between 1948 and 1950 under the 1948 Displaced Persons Act, but he also just met the eligibility cut off.[1] The United States Congress restricted admissions of refugees to those who had entered a refugee camp before December 22, 1945. It was a seemingly neutral date that served to limit Jewish immigration, as many Jews had arrived at the camps after 1945, fleeing post-war pogroms in Poland.[2] David had arrived in Ranshofen barely a month before the deadline.

22

On January 7, 1949, David boarded the S.S. Marine Flasher in Bremerhaven, Germany. David and his fellow 548 passengers were all displaced persons, many of whom were able to immigrate to America thanks to the aid of HIAS.[1] A former C4 United States troopship, the Marine Flasher was daunting in appearance, with a cold metal facade and 523-foot length that was too much to take in at once.[2] The ship was refitted for passengers after a brief stint in the Pacific and used to shuttle immigrants across the Atlantic between 1946 and 1949.[3] The Marine Flasher was bound for Boston, Massachusetts, where David's cousin Benny (Berko's brother Willie's son) was set to meet him.

The trip from Bremerhaven to Boston was a brutal ten days. The upper deck of the ship was barely usable due to the bitter January cold, and the lower decks were packed with hundreds of bunk beds, leaving little space to move around. Exacerbating the conditions were an outbreak of the measles and a violent storm that had taken hold of the North Atlantic.[4] Conditions quickly escalated from some angry seas to a volatile situation, with mountainous waves and winds effortlessly tossing the ship about.

Sea sickness was ubiquitous, even among the experienced crew. For those who were not ill with motion sickness, the pervasive stench of vomit did the trick. The ship nearly capsized off the coast of Newfoundland, tilting to an alarming forty-five-degree angle.[5] The passengers were given an emergency order to return to their bunks,[6] though most were already spending day and night in bed struggling to subdue their nausea and heaving.

Day after day, David remained unbearably dizzy and nauseated. His body viscerally rejected even the slightest bit of food or water. Without any sign of improvement and no prior encounter with motion sickness, he became increasingly convinced that he would not survive the trip, even if the ship did. But after eight horrific days of pounding waves, the ocean finally began to calm.

On January 17, 1949, David watched from the deck as the City of Boston began to materialize. The Marine Flasher pulled into Boston Harbor, damaged and six hours late, but in one piece.[7] David waited in a long line to disembark, where he was processed by customs and immigration authorities. When they asked for David's surname, he told them "Bakst"—the anglicized version of Bakszt that his American relatives were given when they emigrated from Iwje decades earlier.

David Bakst stepped foot on American soil for the first time. The moment was bittersweet. He had finally escaped Europe and embarked on his new life, but his father's presence was markedly absent.

Due to the ship's delayed arrival, Benny Bakst was already waiting at the harbor. Though David and Benny were family and had exchanged letters, the two were virtually strangers. David, knowing no English, was comforted to find that Benny could at least converse with him in broken Yiddish. Benny drove David from Boston to New York City, where their family—Berko's siblings, Willie and Isaac, and their descendants—lived.

David peered out the window as they made their way south, watching as the New York City skyline slowly came into focus. It was a sight to behold. Eventually, they pulled up to Benny's brother's home in Queens, where Leo Bakst and his wife Molly resided.

David was greeted by his large extended family. The day was

exciting not only for David, but also his relatives who had eagerly awaited the arrival of their long-lost relative from Europe. In typical Jewish fashion, Molly Bakst immediately insisted that David eat, placing a plate of food in front of him. David stared at the plate, venturing a small bite. Sensing his hesitation, Molly asked in broken Yiddish, "Do you know what you're eating?"

"No," David answered.

"It's tuna fish."

The transition was challenging, but David embraced his new life in America with vigor. He woke each morning at 4:00 a.m. to commute from Eastern Queens to Williamsburg, Brooklyn, where he worked in his Uncle Willie's pickle and sauerkraut manufacturing business. David spent long days, from dawn to dark, at Bakst Foods, brewing pickle brine by filling large wooden barrels with cucumbers, salt, garlic, dill, and spices and rolling the heavy casks around the factory. Between setting up the barrels and removing jar-ready pickles from them, David's hands were constantly immersed in brine and quickly grew dry and bloated, taking on a sausage-like appearance.

David's few free hours were mostly spent in night school. He viewed learning English as pivotal to fully integrating into American life, and, more urgently, to communicating with his family who spoke little to no Yiddish. David also immediately involved himself with the Jewish community in Queens, attending weekly Shabbat services and joining an Iwje survivor group. His family encouraged him to consider dating within his expanding social circle, but David still pined for Paula. The two had lost contact during their periods of transit, but David hung on to the paper that Paula had given him with Nucham's address in Cuba. "Why do you need a girl from Cuba?" his cousins would moan. "There are plenty of girls here!" But David, settled in New York, decided to write to Paula.

The sentiment was mutual. Paula was giddy to learn that David had safely made it to New York and had not forgotten about her. The two resumed regular letter correspondence, and David set aside a few dollars of his paycheck so he could call her long distance once a week. The couple spoke longingly about being reunited one day, and David promised that he would visit Paula in Havana as soon as he could afford the airfare.

Money was tight, but David saved whatever he could to fund an eventual trip to Cuba. David had been staying in Willie's apartment while his uncle was in Florida for the winter, and once Willie returned the majority of David's weekly earnings went to room and board. Willie arranged for David to move into a spare room in the home of one of his longtime employees who packaged sauerkraut at Bakst Foods. Each night she cooked dinner for her family, always setting a place for David at the table.

In Cuba, Paula's family was supportive of her long-distance romance. Lea, who had come to know David in Ranshofen, thought fondly of the young man. Bushe dragged her niece to a photo studio, insistent that Paula send her boyfriend in America a photograph of herself to keep him interested. Nucham was more skeptical. He had grown protective over Paula, assuming the role of a de facto father. Before allowing David to visit, Nucham demanded that he vet the man.

Nucham flew to New York and found David at the Bakst Foods factory making pickles. It was not the impression David had hoped to make, wearing overalls and reeking of pickle brine in the presence of a well-to-do businessman. The two men discussed David's aspirations for the future, and David was adamant that his days as a low-wage worker were limited. He told Nucham that he was doing what was necessary to make ends meet and adjust to life in America. He planned to ultimately prove his way into a management role.

Rather bluntly, Nucham asked David, "Do you love Paula?"

David answered with an unequivocal "yes." He earned Nucham's blessing.

In November 1949, about three years after he had last seen Paula, David flew to Havana. The Silberfarbs were warm hosts during his three-week stay, and David and Paula immediately fell back into their old rhythm. The couple spent days at the beach and evenings strolling along the streets of Havana hand in hand. As the trip neared its conclusion, David turned to Paula. "Paula, would you want to be my wife?" he asked. She immediately agreed. By the time David boarded the flight back to New York, the couple had decided that David would return in September for their wedding.

Over the following nine months, David continued working in the factory and amassing a small savings. The Silberfarbs spent the time excitedly making wedding arrangements with Nucham generously covering the costs. The couple would be married in a Jewish ceremony at the main synagogue in Havana. David asked his Uncle Willie if he would be willing to attend and escort David down the aisle to the *chuppah*, a role traditionally assumed by the groom's parents. Willie agreed, but as the wedding date approached, he decided that the trip to Cuba would be too onerous on his wife, David's Aunt Rose.

David boarded the plane by himself. As happy as he was to be marrying Paula, he was devastated that none of his own family would be there to celebrate his wedding day with him. When he arrived in Cuba, David and Paula met with the rabbi who would be performing the ceremony. David insisted that the rabbi recite the *El Maleh Rachamim* during the service so that his deceased parents could share in the day. It was an odd request; the prayer is reserved for solemn occasions, such as funerals and *yahrzeits* (anniversaries of deaths). But David was unrelenting and ultimately appeased.

Sensing the young man's distress, Nucham offered to walk David down the aisle with Bushe, leaving Lea and Bernie to escort Paula. David agreed, and in an emotional ceremony, the couple married on September 3, 1950.

The next day, Paula and David flew to Florida on their honeymoon. Uncle Nucham gifted the newlyweds a stay at a lavish beach hotel, and David's cousin, Alvin Bakst, showed them around the area. They returned to New York just in time for the high holidays, spending *Rosh Hashanah* and *Yom Kippur* with Uncle Willie and Aunt Rose.

After the excitement of the wedding and holidays had worn off, David used his savings to find an apartment for him and his wife on 94-46 85th St. in Woodhaven, Queens. The rental was on the fourth floor of a walkup building and so short on space that Paula used the roof to hang dry clothes. But it was a place of their own.

The couple quickly began building a life together. David spent long days in the pickle factory, taking the bus to and from Kent Avenue each day. Paula tended to the home. She proved a responsible manager of the family finances and a talented cook who had dinner ready on the table for David when he returned home each night. After the meal, David and Paula often rode the bus together to their English classes, and they quickly became fluent in the language. The pair kept a kosher home, observed the Sabbath strictly, and regularly attended prayer services. Within a year, Paula was pregnant.

PHOTOS

David Bakszt at Berko Bakszt's grave in Hofgeismar, Germany, December 1948.

Left to right: Batya Bakszt, Rochelle Bialobroda, Fishel Bialobroda. Tel Aviv, Israel, 1948.

Paula Silberfarb and her cousin Simon Rozen in Havana, Cuba, late 1940s.

Left to right: Sophia Silberfarb and Paula Silberfarb. Havana, Cuba, 1949.

The photo Paula Silberfarb sent to David Bakst of herself. Havana, Cuba, early 1949.

Left to right: Paula Silberfarb, David Bakst, Nucham Rozen. Havana, Cuba, 1949.

Left to right: David Bakst, Paula Silberfarb, Lea Silberfarb at David and Paula's wedding. Havana, Cuba, September 3, 1950.

David Bakst and Paula Silberfarb at their wedding. Havana, Cuba, September 3, 1950.

David Bakst and Paula Bakst in the early 1950s, New York.

Willie Bakst and Rose Bakst, location and date unknown.

23

In Israel, Batya felt at home. She fell in love with the burgeoning country, celebrating in the streets of Tel Aviv when the nation declared independence and fighting with a rifle in the 1948 Arab-Israeli War. Batya found solace in her Jewish community and went back to school to become a kindergarten teacher. She had a knack for languages and earned extra money to support her family by translating Russian literature into Hebrew.

But Batya quickly became acquainted with another side of Fishel. He had a temper that flared up quickly and violently. After being left bruised and beaten on multiple occasions, Batya, concerned for her own safety and that of her daughter, decided she had to escape the marriage. Under Jewish law that governed in Israel, dissolving a marital union required that the husband provide the wife with a *get*, or writ of divorce. Fishel would not agree to a *get*, holding Batya hostage in her own marriage.

Batya was well read and understood that she could obtain a civil divorce if she immigrated to America. Sacrificing her deep desire to remain in Israel, Batya persuaded Fishel that they should move to the United States, where they could obtain citizenship through David's sponsorship and live without the constant fear that another Arab-Israeli war might break out. Fishel agreed. The pair decided that Batya would travel to America first, file the necessary paperwork, and then arrange for her husband and daughter to join her.

Batya left Israel by ship to stay with David and Paula in May 1956. She worked odd jobs to support herself while she wound her way through the United States immigration system. After a few weeks, she was able to secure a room in a small house, where she cooked and cleaned for the owner in exchange for reduced rent.

Meanwhile, as he waited for his wife to send for him, Fishel abandoned nine-year-old Rochelle in a *kibbutz*, visiting only on rare occasions. *Kibbutzim* were socialist communities in Israel where members typically worked for the same pay, ate in communal dining halls, and placed their offspring in designated children's homes. Separated from her parents in one of these children's centers, Rochelle was miserable and confused. She cried herself to sleep each night until her father finally returned to take her to America in late 1956.

Batya arranged for Rochelle and Fishel to travel by ship to America. She understood that she could have filed the visa paperwork only on behalf of Rochelle, freeing herself from Fishel permanently, but Batya remained true to her word and applied for her husband as well. Fishel arrived in New York expecting a warm greeting from his wife. Instead, he was met with a stack of divorce papers. "I don't want to be married to you anymore," Batya said matter-of-factly as she handed him the paperwork.

Sol Feder, a local glazer, and David became acquainted through a mutual friend. Sol had suffered through his own share of horrors during the Holocaust. He was one of eight children born to a dirt-poor Jewish family in Frampol, Poland, and he struggled to keep himself and his siblings alive by hiding in sewers, barns, and forest swamps. The Poles in his town—religious Catholics—were particularly cruel to the Jews, tormenting the Feders and repeatedly reporting their hideouts to the Nazis. Of the ten-person family, only Sol and one other brother survived, the others meeting torturous deaths by Nazi gunfire and the gas chambers of Bergen-Belsen.

Sol was an attractive and well-off man with a thick European accent, contagious smile, and reputation as being a bit of a Casanova. Sol impressed in his car, a luxury that many survivors, including the Baksts, could not afford. His male friends enjoyed going out with him, having their pick of the many women Sol rejected.

During one of Sol's frequent trips to the Bakst home, his car got a flat tire. Batya, over at the house visiting, stepped outside to help Sol. She lay down on the driveway and began changing the tire, knowing full well which tools to use and how. Sol was dumbfounded. No woman he knew would get her hands dirty performing car repairs. He immediately began pursuing Batya.

Batya had little interest. While she took English classes at Jamaica High School to better learn the local language, Sol attended so he could pick up attractive Swedish women. Batya was focused on earning a teaching certification so she could work at a Hebrew school. But Sol was undeterred and eventually wore her down.

The couple began seriously dating, and Fishel—still formally married to Batya—discovered that Sol was a frequent overnight guest at Batya's apartment. When he next came over to visit with Rochelle, Fishel showed up in a fit of rage. He opened Batya's closet and cut holes in the breast and crotch regions of all her clothing.

Though she was happy with Sol, Batya lived in terror of Fishel. Through her Jewish network, she had learned of an opportunity to work as a Hebrew teacher at a large synagogue in Miami, Florida. Batya jumped at the chance to escape New York and moved herself and Rochelle down South.

Batya excelled at teaching and quickly became responsible for managing lesson planning for the entire Hebrew school. Though the job was not intended to support a family and Batya and Rochelle barely lived above the poverty line, it was the happiest Batya had been in years. She had full custody of her daughter and felt safe. The two spent all of their free time together, playing outside and sharing homemade sandwiches at the nearby movie theater.

By putting physical distance between herself and Sol, Batya

only increased Sol's interest in being with her. He was not inclined to settle down, but Sol had also grown to truly love Batya. She was different from the other women he surrounded himself with; she worked outside the house voluntarily, was well read, and was an outspoken Zionist. Sol knew that he never would have had a chance to be with a woman like Batya in Frampol. He flew down to Florida several times to visit Batya, and after her civil divorce was finally processed, they married in March 1959.

24

Outwardly, David and Paula Bakst were the poster family for the American dream. Their daughter Rochelle, named for David's mother Rochel, was born on March 3, 1952. Paula's mother and sister flew in from Cuba almost immediately to offer assistance for several weeks. David worked long days and weekends, struggling to make rent let alone take his wife out on a date or buy his daughter a toy. Receiving a mere piece of sidewalk chalk was a special occasion for Rochelle.

But just as he had planned, David climbed the corporate hierarchy. He went from pushing pickle barrels to loading delivery trucks with the forklift to supervising other employees packaging Bakst Foods products. David and his wife became naturalized citizens, and David in particular developed a strong affection for his country and the freedoms it offered.

Paula was careful not to squander David's earnings on frivolous spending, though she understood the value in investing in high-quality products. She cooked kosher meat from the butcher and made soups and salads with fresh vegetables, reminiscent of the meals the couple ate as children in Europe. Thanks to Paula's diligent budgeting, within a few years the family was able to rent a small home in Ozone Park, Queens.

But Paula was barely twenty when she gave birth. Though the war had forced them to grow up, Paula and David were still children themselves, struggling to deal with the trauma of their stolen adolescences. At night, Paula woke not just to feed the baby but screaming from her own nightmares. When she walked around the neighborhood, Paula went the long way to avoid crossing in front of a neighbor's yard out of fear that his docile German Shepard—the same breed of dog used by the Nazis—might attack her.

Beyond their familial relationships, the Baksts' main source of companionship was with other Eastern European immigrants. Holocaust survivor groups cropped up in New York City, and the couple met and reconnected with several friends. David's distant cousin Moshe Baran and his wife Malka—a Hasag Labor Camp survivor—settled in Queens and were frequent Shabbat dinner guests. Paula grew friendly with Judy, whose mother, Bashke Fialkov, had been forced to smother her own baby in the forest during the war. The Bakst home was regularly filled with survivors whose coping mechanisms were to discuss the atrocities they had witnessed.

The environment was inhospitable for a young girl. Rochelle Bakst listened to stories of Nazi killing fields and mass exterminations, unwittingly absorbing her parents' anxieties. She suffered from chronic nightmares, always jolting awake the moment before the Nazi haunting her subconscious managed to shoot her. Rochelle grew terrified of bedtime and fiercely fought her drooping eyelids to delay the inevitable horror.

In October 1956, Paula gave birth to a son. The next day, Lea and Sophia appeared on the Baksts' doorstep again, this time with permanent visas. Steven, named after his grandfather Samuel Silberfarb, quickly proved to be a precocious child whom David and Paula struggled to rear. His toddler days hit at a stressful time for the Baksts. David took on a leadership role at work, helping grow Bakst Foods into the cold-cuts industry, and was kept away from the home for the bulk of each day. Paula was left to watch two kids and manage an overcrowded household, which now also included her mother and sister. Having a child who was constantly climbing out of enclosures and wandering off was a continual source of frustration for David and Paula. Desperate to keep Steven confined, David tied him into his crib and playpen with rope, which on at least one occasion resulted in Steven escaping halfway down the block, donning a rope harness with a playpen in tow.

Like Rochelle, Steven was exposed to the war's atrocities at a young age. On weekend mornings when Bashke and Judy came to visit, he often had to warn his Bubby Lea that Bashke was out on the front stoop in her slip. The woman was kindhearted but plainly broken by her experience in the forests of Poland. She became increasingly paranoid, muttering absurdities to herself and telling the Bakst children that her son-in-law was trying to poison her.

On the way to the grocery store, Paula told her five-year-old son about the mass killing in Serniki. The walk from the parking lot into Daitch Shopwell was a blur to Steven as he struggled to process what his mother had just said to him. While they waited at the deli counter, the boy turned to his mother. "What did you mean by the ground was still moving?" Steven asked. Paula explained that the Nazis did not have enough bullets to kill everyone and many Jews were buried alive. For years, Steven could not shake the vision of his ancestors lying half dead in a pit, covered in dirt. He often found himself wondering what he would have done if he were alive at the time.

Sophia Silberfarb seemed more skilled at compartmentalizing and quickly took to life in New York City. As an attractive woman in her twenties, she had suitors regularly knocking on the door of the Bakst home. She spent hours each weekend primping in the home's single bathroom before slipping into a low-cut dress and spending the night out dancing. Sophia quickly captured the heart of a good-natured Holocaust survivor who worked as a jeweler in Manhattan. He wanted desperately to marry Sophia. But she remained preoccupied with a local American-born typesetter named Marvin Bressler.

As Sophia and Marvin's relationship grew serious, Lea implored her daughter not to marry him. She sensed that Sophia was choosing a man based on looks, not substance. "He's a statue!" became such a common refrain around the house that little Steven thought his aunt was marrying an actual statue. Sophia disregarded her mother's advice, and in 1959, she and Marvin wed and moved to a small home on the corner of Brookville Boulevard and 147th Avenue in Rosedale, Queens.

Lea Silberfarb, still living with Paula and David, became like a second mother in the Bakst home. She kept an eye on Steven and Rochelle, cleaned the house, and assisted Paula in the kitchen. Lea and David also developed a sweet relationship. Both read The Forward in Yiddish each day and regularly discussed current events and politics. David respected Lea immensely, and though small in stature, she was the only person in the household with the power to trump the patriarch. When David was debating purchasing a home for the family after his son Gary—named for Gershon Silberfarb—was born in 1959, it was Lea who convinced him to pull the trigger. David agonized over the price tag until Lea sat him down. "You can do this," she said. "We all have faith in you."

255-02 Memphis Avenue in Rosedale, Queens was a modest, two-family home in a largely working-class Jewish and Italian neighborhood. It was located just a few blocks from the children's school and had a small yard where David taught Gary to hit a baseball. Though American sports were initially foreign to David, he became a dedicated fan. David avidly watched Mets games and joined the local Rosedale Jewish Center's bowling league. He played weekly games and quickly became competitive, winning tournaments with scores well into the two hundreds.

Paula filled the new home with the scent of her traditional cooking. One could sense whether a holiday was approaching based on the level of frenzy in her kitchen. Paula and Lea spent days preparing for holiday meals. On Passover, after deep cleaning the kitchen and switching out the dishware, they made their own gefilte fish from a blend of pike, whitefish, and carp. Paula visited a Brooklyn fish market, identifying precisely which fish she wanted from a massive tank as a frustrated store clerk wildly waved around a net until he scooped up the rights ones. Paula took the fish home whole, using the bones and skin to make broth. The carp, hardy fish, were usually still alive by the time Paula returned and were left to swim in the family's single bathtub, sometimes for over a day. On at least one occasion, Steven took a shower as a carp swam around his feet.

The Baksts hosted elaborate seders for their extended family, which stretched late into the night. David led the seders, ensuring that every prayer was recited in full and explaining its meaning for those who were less fluent in Hebrew. After the meal, he and Sophia sang the Passover songs together with pride, entertaining the family with beautiful music and overwhelming joy.

Each Friday evening, Paula cooked Shabbat dinner like her mother had in Serniki. She made salad, matzo ball soup, and chicken; lit the ritual candles; and plopped a kiss on each of her children's foreheads while wishing them a *Shabbat Shalom*. David sang the prayers, giving his wife and each child a blessing before reciting the *kiddush* over the wine and *motzei* over the challah bread.

In the morning, the Baksts donned their suits and dresses for services. The *shomer Shabbat* family did not drive or use electric during the Sabbath, so they walked the half mile to the Rosedale Jewish Center where Saturday services and thrice-weekly Hebrew school lessons were held.

Though a significant Jewish population lived in the area, antisemitism was still prevalent. The temple had been the target of hate crimes, as had many others in the area. In one instance, vandals smashed a cellar window, climbed into the Rosedale Jewish Center, and desecrated a Torah.[1] They tore up portions of the holy scroll and wrote obscenities on it, shattered a showcase of religious objects from Israel, and ripped up prayer books.[2] At school, the Bakst children knew to keep their heads down, accustomed to finding swastikas drawn on their desks or being called "kikes."

Rochelle Bakst in particular longed to fit in with the regular Americans at school who ate normal foods and dressed stylishly rather than in mismatched or hand-me-down clothes. Sharing a room with her Bubby Lea from the old country did not fit

Rochelle's desired persona, and the two sometimes clashed. Despite being less assimilated than Paula, Lea was extraordinarily astute. She was the only one in the household not blissfully ignorant to Rochelle's teenage antics, recognizing immediately that the girl's telephone discussions of "going to the candy store" were coded references to drug experimentation.

Paula's constant worry that something might happen to her children also hindered Rochelle's desire for independence. If Rochelle asked to do anything, Paula's default answer was "we'll see," which was as good as a "no." On summer Sundays, when David took the family to Rockaway Beach in Queens, Paula, encumbered by a lifelong fear of water, found some excuse why the children could not go swimming; the ocean was cold, or they were about to eat, or they had just had lunch. David, meanwhile, happily sat on the shore unabashedly blasting Jo Amar, a Moroccan-Israeli singer.

Paula's fears also made her a deeply devoted parent. She showered the children with love and attention, ensuring that all of their needs were met. When Steven came down with the chickenpox, Paula sat at his bedside until he was fully recovered, rubbing his back and talking to him for hours to keep him entertained. She trekked by bus to Jamaica, Queens, to buy the children woolen clothes, not wanting them to suffer in the winter cold like she did in the forest.

David, too, went out of his way to spend time with his family. Even with his work demands, David was home for family dinners each night and dedicated Sundays to his children. When they were not at the beach, he took the Baksts for picnics in Brookville Park, hamburgers at Wetson's, or rides at Nunley's Amusement Park. And while most other neighborhood kids were left to walk or take public transportation to their social outings at the movies or the mall, David insisted on giving his children a ride there and back, no matter the hour.

25

In Cuba, civil unrest was growing as Fidel Castro consolidated power and propagated his communist regime. Although Castro's policies never specifically targeted Jews, the American trade embargo and Cuba's nationalization of businesses posed a particular threat to Cuban Jews who primarily made their livings by running small businesses.[1] Havana went from having a bustling Jewish community of more than 15,000 Jews and five synagogues to a near Jewish ghost town.[2]

The decision to leave was a difficult one for Bernie Silberfarb, the Rozens, and the Milners. Not only were they leaving their homeland and businesses behind, but with much of their wealth tied up in inventory, they were also abandoning a large portion of their livelihoods. Bernie decided to head north to stay with Paula in New York. He had started a successful business in Cuba—far more robust than Nucham's fabric shop—and was determined to do the same in America. With only $500 in his pocket, Bernie arrived on the steps of the Bakst home. The other relatives moved to Florida, where many Cuban Jews relocated.

Bernie purchased a van and started buying and reselling closeouts. He was a cunning businessman and adapted quickly to operating in the States. On one occasion he bought name-brand batteries in bulk from the manufacturer, claiming he qualified for a significant clockmaker discount that required him to include a battery in each clock he sold. Bernie placed the batteries in boxes similar to the manufacturer's packaging and resold them at a massive margin. Soon enough, Bernie's antics had him living on his own and filling Paula and David's garage and basement with ceiling-high stacks of boxes of inventory.

Bernie had a magnetic personality. He commanded the attention of a room the moment he stepped inside, and those around him constantly craved his approval. Though Bernie visited far less frequently than a son should and typically unannounced, when he did show up, Lea and the Baksts fawned over his presence. They showered him with attention and ran around the kitchen in a frenzy, fixing him a glass of scotch and a plate of the best food they could find.

Steven admired Bernie less for his personality and more for his business acumen. From a young age, Steven had a knack for business and mechanics. He frequently accompanied David to the Bakst Foods warehouse, steering his first forklift at the age of five and fully operating it as soon as his feet could reach the pedal. By the end of elementary school, Steven was visiting the warehouse every weekend with his father, checking that the refrigeration trucks were properly cooling stored cold cuts and eventually sneaking off to practice driving David's car around the parking lot.

Steven's technical skills, though impressive, were often unappreciated. At nine years old, Steven hid a wire underneath the carpet from a radio in his closet, which he had adapted into a microphone. He ran the wire down the hall and under Rochelle's bed, where it connected to a small speaker hidden inside a shoebox. When Rochelle returned to her room after a shower, Steven whispered, "Rochelle, I see you" into the microphone. After repeatedly rushing into Rochelle's room in response to her screams, David eventually found the hidden wire and traced it back to find Steven giggling in his closet. On another occasion, the boy cut open one of Rochelle's old stuffed animals, installed lights in its eyes, and wired it to the family car's blinkers. The toy dog sat on the rear deck of the car, its corresponding eye flashing whenever the right or left blinker was activated.

Both times, as in many others, David beat Steven for his shenanigans. Steven struggled with undiagnosed attention deficit hyperactivity disorder (ADHD). Unable to compete with his siblings academically and often misbehaved, he was made the scapegoat of the Bakst household. When Gary developed a lingering cough, David said it was because Steven teased him too much. Indeed, Steven teased his siblings mercilessly, prodding them underneath the dinner table and ruining school projects. But David's negative reactions only reaped more negative behaviors. Each night inevitably ended with David, exhausted from a long day at work, losing his temper at the dinner table and chasing Steven around the house with a belt.

Paula was more patient. When Steven struggled to memorize the New York City bridges, she sat with him for hours coming up with mnemonics to help him pass the test. Though she feared driving, Paula even got her license so that she could continue taking English and mathematics classes and help her kids learn to read and memorize multiplication tables. But Paula was nine years her husband's junior and raising children in the 1960s; traditional gender roles permeated the household. While Paula was happy to indulge Steven's interest in cooking with her, that ended when David noticed and dragged the boy out of the kitchen by his ear.

Steven had two sources of solace. The first was his Bubby, Lea. Lea understood the problematic family dynamic and when tensions boiled, she physically forced herself between David and Steven. She knew David would never lay a hand on her. At night, Lea let Steven crawl into bed with her, cuddling him while sweetly singing in Yiddish until he felt safe.

Steven's other solace was shadowing his Uncle Bernie at Bernie's health and beauty aid distribution company. Steven was thrilled to learn from his uncle's genius—albeit in hindsight likely fraudulent—schemes. He worked in Bernie's small, and eventually much larger, warehouse, eagerly completing whatever ridiculous tasks his uncle asked of him. After elementary school let out,

Steven spent hours with a small makeup brush gluing name-brand hairspray labels onto knock-off canisters until he unwittingly grew high off the contact cement. He and other workers used acetone to dissolve "for hospital use only" and "not for resale" warnings off products. Another time, the grade-school-aged child was tasked with driving Bernie's Cadillac back to his house.

Steven watched in awe as his uncle played sellers against each other and manipulated those he had swindled into apologizing, including, once, the senior vice president of Colgate-Palmolive. When Certs rolled out its line of specked mints, Bernie bought up the old, unspeckled product, leaving it to sit for years in the back corner of his warehouse. Every time Steven reminded his uncle that the product was languishing, Bernie waved the boy away. "Don't worry about it," he would say. Years later, Bernie convinced Certs to buy back the trailer loads of "defective" mints at the end-seller's price under threat of releasing the long-expired product onto the market. Soon enough, Bernie was a millionaire with a wife and kids out on Long Island.

26

Several nights per week the phone at the Bakst house rang, and, like clockwork, David climbed out of bed and drove the one-mile distance to Sophia's house. Marvin had a bad temper that would inevitably flare up and leave Sophia calling over to her sister's home in fear. Usually Marvin failed to act on his threats, but from time to time his anger boiled into physical abuse against his terrorized wife and children.

David would show up at the Bressler home, wedge himself between Sophia and Marvin, and attempt to deescalate the situation. On one occasion, David found Marvin strangling one of his sons. On another, David insisted that Steven accompany him to the Bressler home. When they arrived at the house, David walked over to Marvin, who towered above him. David gestured aggressively at his chest. "You pick on me, you coward!" he shouted. Marvin pushed David, David shoved back, and the encounter erupted into a fistfight in front of the horrified bystanders.

After these altercations Sophia often returned to the Bakst home with David, staying from hours to weeks. When she did, Sophia brought her daughter Muriel, not wanting to leave the youngster alone with Marvin. Muriel was a sweet and clever girl who suffered some developmental delays due to a presumed oxygen deprivation at birth. Marvin had no use for a daughter, let alone a daughter with special needs, and he treated her the cruelest of the family's three children. Muriel grew fearful of her father and spent most of her days holed up in her cubical-sized bedroom, looking out her single window across Brookville Boulevard into the park.

Rochelle and Steven came to resent their aunt's frequent visits. Lea, Bernie, and the Baksts had been telling Sophia for years to leave Marvin, but nothing ever changed. Space was limited in the Rosedale home, and Sophia's constant presence was an inconvenience, especially once Doreen Bakst was born in 1967. The Bakst children were often forced to give up their beds so their aunt and cousin had a place to sleep. Yet, whenever the phone rang, David reliably came to his sister-in-law's aid.

Between Sophia's calls, parenting four kids, and his own career, David was constantly busy. Willie had retired, and Bakst Foods—now called Mirobe—was being run out of a warehouse in Saint Albans, Queens, by Willie's son, Irving, and less-involved grandson, Michael, with David as third in command.

Irving made sourcing cold cuts into larger grocers a priority, but his calls to companies such as King Kullen and Shopwell went unanswered. Given Irving's larger-than-life personality and willingness to engage with the seedier aspects of New York, it was foreseeable that the solution to his predicament would come in the form of an influential Italian man who controlled much of the city's kosher meat industry.

The man promised Irving that, in exchange for a substantial stake in the company and a hefty weekly payment, Mirobe would have unfettered access to virtually any supermarket in the tri-state area. Irving was skeptical. "We've tried. They won't take our calls," he explained.

"Trust me," the man said, "just call them."

The two men agreed, and suddenly the supermarkets were eager to deal with Mirobe. The deal bought the company a near monopoly over cold-cut distribution in the New York metropolitan region.

David managed the entire supply side of Mirobe, which was suddenly booming. He was responsible for ordering the perishable products from vendors, ensuring that they remained properly cooled, and allocating them between nearly a dozen delivery trucks to fulfill orders from hundreds grocery stores and bodegas. David also handled the company's cash, and though he had unfettered access, never once took an extra penny for himself. David was unflaggingly honest. When he came home from work and discovered that Steven took a couple of cinderblocks from a construction site in New Jersey, David drove the boy all the way back to return the pilfered property.

It was unsurprising then that David was less than keen about his new responsibility for coordinating weekly payments for Tommy and Nicki, representatives of Mirobe's newest silent partner. When they arrived to collect on Friday afternoons in their suits and company-issued Cadillacs, David always had their money ready and dutifully showed them around the warehouse when asked. David's reliability and reluctance to ask questions about their connections to multiple crime families led Tommy and Nicki to regard him well, and the pair became a useful contact when David found himself occasionally in need of assistance.

In addition to his anger management issues, Marvin Bressler had developed a gambling addiction. He was constantly pursued by Italian bookies who had no qualms about approaching his family to collect on the debts. One night, Sophia awoke at three in the morning to find the family car engulfed in flames as it sat parked in the driveway. Each time the collectors came knocking, Bernie bailed out Marvin, giving his sister the money to pay off the debts to keep her and her children safe.

Bernie even offered to support Sophia if she divorced Marvin. But Sophia lacked the resolve to do so, leaving Bernie and David increasingly concerned about her security. David, with the assistance of his Mirobe contacts, orchestrated a meeting with the bookies. The men met Sophia and Bernie at the Pizza King near Sophia's home, a known hangout spot on 147th Avenue and Brookville Boulevard. Bernie proposed a deal: he would pay off

Marvin's five-figure debt if the bookies vowed not to go after Sophia or her children when Marvin inevitably accrued future liabilities. The men agreed and kept their word.

In the 1960s, the second wave of the feminist movement took hold in America. Batya was not only a supporter but also an embodiment of it. She marched by the beat of her own drum, wearing Indian saris and becoming close friends with a German Lutheran neighbor in a community where Jews only associated with other Jews. While her female counterparts played cards and socialized, Batya spent her time reading Dostoyevsky and Gandhi, practicing her impressionist-style painting technique, protesting the Vietnam War, and earning a teaching certification from Cornell University.

One of the means by which Sol persuaded Batya to move back to New York was purchasing a home for the two of them and Batya's daughter across the street from the Rosedale Jewish Center. Batya was immediately hired as a Hebrew school teacher at the temple, and before long she became the first female principal of the Hebrew school. Batya was deeply passionate about the role, believing that learning Hebrew was integral to raising a generation of Zionist, rather than simply Jewish, Americans. The children adored her, engaged by the warm environment she fostered.

In addition to her day job and traveling to New Jersey to teach adult Hebrew classes, Batya played a major role in managing Feder Glass. Sol was a competent glazier, using their home's garage on the corner of Francis Lewis Boulevard and 247th Street as his workshop. But Sol's failure to pay attention in English classes left him hindered; he was functionally illiterate and completely reliant on Batya to manage the company's finances and marketing.

In the early 1960s, Sol's neighbor—Henry Hill—knocked on the door wanting to speak to Sol about his business. "How do you get your work?" Henry asked. Sol answered that he advertised in the paper and hung flyers. "And how do you get paid?" Henry questioned. Sol told Henry he was charging $5 per window. "Okay," Henry said, "I'll get you paid $7, you give me the extra $2, and I'll find you more work." Seeing no downside, Sol agreed.

For a one-man shop, Feder Glass became a prosperous business. Henry funneled plenty of customers Sol's way, tasking him with glazing much of the borough of Staten Island. Henry's customers all paid promptly and in cash.

Around the same time, Batya began insisting that she and Sol have a baby. Sol was wholly uninterested in bringing a child into the world, believing that another Holocaust was just around the corner. But Batya was adamant, and after years of trying to get pregnant, she gave birth to Ben Feder in 1964.

Sol, assuming Batya would leave her job after giving birth, was shocked to learn that she intended to continue running the Hebrew school. "We have enough money," Sol said. "I don't want you going back to work." It was not an option that Batya was willing to entertain. She returned to Rosedale Jewish Center, either bringing baby Ben along with her or leaving him home with hired help.

Though Batya did not look for fights, her brashness certainly ruffled feathers. She was outgoing and unabashed in sharing her views on Israel and politics, often the only woman socializing in a group of men. Men were stunned when their racist remarks were met with a detailed explanation of why American society was discriminatory. "If we allow this, what's the difference between us and Germany?" she emphatically questioned. When altercations made the evening news, Batya would point to the television and ask her husband, "Do you think that would happen to a white person?"

David, though less outspoken, also recognized parallels between Nazism and racism in America. After returning from a business trip down South, he lamented that a Black man felt compelled to step off the sidewalk and into the street gutter as David passed him. "I escaped Europe to see this?" It was one of the few instances where David was critical of America.

Both David and Batya remained devout Jews, but Batya took issue with the gender inequalities in the religion. She was a relentless advocate for women's right to fully participate in services, insisting that they be given *aliyas*, the honor of reciting the blessing for a Torah reading traditionally reserved for men.

The Conservative Jewish movement was then unwilling to

accommodate such progressivism. Batya frequently clashed with the rabbi at her synagogue, who was unhappy that a woman was leading the Hebrew school, let alone expressing opinions on religious inclusivity. Batya's efforts were aggressively shunned by temple leadership and, to her particular disappointment, fellow female congregants.

Even Paula was reluctant to support her sister-in-law's efforts. Paula was far less willing to challenge societal norms and never quite warmed to Batya. She viewed Batya as uppity and, perhaps correctly, sensed that Batya thought Paula was never fully deserving of David.

In the spring of 1974, David underwent invasive prostate surgery. The procedure required an extended recovery period and led to much anxiety in the Bakst household. Rochelle Bakst, having graduated from college and moved to the West Coast, boarded a hippie bus cross country to help pick up the slack at home while Paula cared for David. Before David left for the hospital, Lea gave her son-in-law a hug. "If something should happen, let it happen to me, not you," she whispered to him as he departed.

When Rochelle Bakst walked into the house in Rosedale, she found Lea in the kitchen making dinner for herself and Doreen. Lea was putting steaks into the oven still wrapped in freezer paper. "Bubby, you can't put them in the oven like that," Rochelle said. To Rochelle's surprise, Lea insisted that she was cooking them correctly. After a protracted back-and-forth, Rochelle screamed out in frustration, "You're going to burn the house down, Bubby!" Finally, Lea had a moment of clarity and realized her mistake.

Lea's absentmindedness swiftly worsened, and she began experiencing painful headaches. David was still in the hospital when Lea was diagnosed with an incurable and aggressive malignant brain tumor. One day she turned to Steven, who was nearly of age. "When I die, I don't want you to cry for me," she said. Steven spent the better part of the day sobbing in the basement.

Though her condition was set to decline rapidly, Lea refused to go to the hospital and instead continued puttering around the house, leaving stoves and electronics on in her wake. But sensing something was acutely wrong one day, Lea instructed her daughter, "Paula, take me to the hospital. If something should happen to me, I don't want you to have on your conscience that you could have done something."

Suddenly, Paula found her mother and husband in two different hospitals. Lea had brain surgery to remove the tumor, but it grew back quickly. The hospital could do little to help the decompensating woman and discharged her with the recommendation that she be placed in an elder care facility. Bernie, over his mother's objections, took Lea to a nursing home in the Bronx.

Paula was adamant that David should not be told about Lea until he progressed further in his recovery. The surgery was a success, but David was already struggling post-operatively with unrelenting hiccups, pain, and blood clots, and Paula knew that he would be crippled by the news. Batya disagreed. She insisted that her brother had a right to know and took it upon herself to inform him over Paula's objections.

As predicted, David was devastated by Lea's diagnosis, haunted by her final words to him before his surgery. The hospital called Paula that night, concerned that David's grief was taking a toll on his health. His vitals declined and he was hyperventilating so heavily that the hospital had to put him on a Valium regimen for several days. Though David ultimately recuperated, Batya's visit set his recovery back substantially and exacerbated the existing cleavage between her and her sister-in-law.

Paula and Rochelle Bakst shouldered the entire burden of care, alternating between sitting with Lea in the Bronx and David in Queens. Sophia visited occasionally and Bernie even less. "What can I do about it?" Bernie would say to Steven when confronted about his lack of visits. "I'd pay anything to fix it if I could." As Lea grew non-verbal, Rochelle became concerned that the staff at the facility were not treating the frail women with sufficient care and guarded her Bubby closely. When one of the workers bumped Lea's leg into the bed as he scooped her up, the ordinarily docile

Rochelle shrieked at him, seeing the pain in her grandmother's eyes.

Even when Lea lost consciousness, Rochelle or Paula continued to visit daily. Paula struggled to make the painful decision to let her mother go, and Lea remained on a feeding tube for months before she slipped away on August 10, 1974. The family was distraught, but true to his word, Steven forced himself not to cry. Lea was seventy-three years old when she died, living with the Baksts from the time Steven was born until just weeks before he started college.

27

Sol never gave his wife the intellectual stimulation she craved, but their relationship was physically intense. At the end of the day, they embraced passionately, and the couple became famous in the local community for their dancing at weddings and bar mitzvahs. At one event, they became so engrossed in the tango that every other couple migrated to the dance-floor sidelines to watch.

Sol did not dare raise a hand to his wife, but like Fishel, he was deeply scarred by his past. He was not formally educated and spent much of his teenage years in hiding, entirely deprived of proper socialization. He never learned how to appropriately talk to his wife or raise children and was frequently verbally abusive and financially controlling over Batya. Batya did her best to defy Sol's orders—she continued taking painting classes in Manhattan over his objections—but his control over the purse strings often left her wanting. She begged her husband to purchase a home for them in Caesarea, Israel, longing to return, but Sol refused.

Sol treated Rochelle like a second-class child in their home, never fully considering her to be his own daughter. When she sought to apply to college after graduating from high school, Sol refused to pay. With Ben, Sol often let his temper get the better of himself, and disagreements devolved into blows. Batya, a pioneer for women's rights outside the home, never quite learned how to handle the man inside her own home.

Rochelle was eager to get away from Sol. She pursued several degrees in nursing and moved in with an older woman, tending to the household in exchange for rent. Then she met Norman. Norman was a kind and simple man. He ran a storage and delivery company with his father and treated Rochelle well but was otherwise uninspiring. Batya's attempts to persuade her daughter not to make the same mistake that she had made fell on deaf ears; Rochelle and Norman wed, adopted a son named Larry, and moved to a house in Syosset.

Ben's childhood bedroom overlooked the garage where Sol kept his workshop. One day he noticed a group of men walking into the garage. "Dad, people are in your workshop!" he shouted frantically.

Sol dismissed the boy's concerns summarily. "Don't worry about it."

Over time, Ben came to recognize the men who frequently held meetings in the Feder garage: Henry Hill and his associates.

Henry lived three doors down and was generally friendly and well liked in the community. He was kind enough to Ben and respected Batya. "Your mother is a good woman, Benny," he would say to Ben. Nobody but the Hills called Ben "Benny."

When Ben's yeshiva had students sell kosher Barton's candy as a fundraiser, Ben went door-to-door trying to entice his neighbors to purchase a box or two. Henry answered the door, and Ben asked whether he wanted to buy some candy.

"Benny, why are you selling this?" Henry asked.

"I win a basketball if I sell $100 worth, Mr. Hill," Ben explained.

Henry reached into his pocket and pulled out the thickest roll of cash Ben had ever seen, wrapped in a fat rubber band. Ben's eyes widened. "Here, go buy the fucking basketball!" Henry slapped a $100 bill into the boy's hand. Before Ben could even muster a "thank you," Henry had shut the front door.

Ben ran home, eager to get the $100 bill to safety. When he told his mother what had transpired, Batya insisted that they fill out a candy order for Henry. She and Ben sat at the table as Batya diligently scanned the order list for items that her neighbor might like. "I'm sure Mr. Hill would like kosher peanut brittle," she announced, checking off the box. Batya checked off box after box until there were no more boxes left to check. She had ordered every product available, and the order still only totaled $92. Twenty minutes later, she sent Ben back to bring Mr. Hill his change.

When the candy arrived weeks later, Henry's order was too large for Ben to carry on his own. Batya helped him schlep the four giant bags down the street and left Ben at the front door to deliver them.

Karen Hill answered the door. "Benny, what is all this?" she asked, looking down at the boy surrounded by bags.

"Mr. Hill bought it for my school fundraiser."

Karen turned around, leaving the door wide open as she shouted into the house. "Henry, did you order all this shit?"

As Sol and David grew increasingly financially comfortable, they began spending more time upstate with their families. David and Paula went from renting a bungalow a few weeks per year to staying the entire summer in the Catskills. The Borscht Belt was known for its bungalow colonies and all-inclusive hotels catering to Jews escaping New York City's summer heat. The adults filled their days sitting outside, playing cards, and watching shows. The children went to camp.

Early Monday mornings David made the several-hour drive in his company Cadillac back to the city for the workweek and returned late Friday nights. Irving Bakst had retired, and with his son, Michael Bakst, largely preoccupied by addiction, David was running Mirobe. The company further expanded beyond pickled goods and deli meats, sourcing major products like Marie's salad dressing and Jimmy Dean sausages. David oversaw the several-thousand-square-foot warehouse and fifteen refrigeration trucks that each carried over $20,000 in inventory to roughly 800 stores in the tri-state area.

At work and in the community, David built a reputation for himself. Even on weekends he was frequently at the Mirobe warehouse, checking to make sure that the trucks were properly cooling the perishable products stored inside. When the building's alarm went off, he rushed over, no matter the hour. After a rash of burglary attempts, David prepared a box of assorted cold cuts for the reporting officers. It was both a kind and cunning gesture; whenever the alarm sounded thereafter, David knew that the police would promptly respond to the call.

To his children's amazement, David was greeted warmly at the local breakfast spot in Laurelton, where the staff already knew his order. He was also a leader within the Holocaust survivor community. David kept the Iwje survivor group alive, arranging annual meetings while Paula ran the organization's books. When members fell on hard times, David quietly brought them food for their families.

Even amongst the extended Bakst-Silberfarb family, David was treated as the patriarch. When Batya's son-in-law, Norman, got into a scuffle with distributors at work, his wife, Rochelle, called Uncle David for assistance. David had one conversation with Tommy and the situation was resolved. And though Sol Feder never considered Norman and Rochelle's son to be his grandson—Larry was "his stepdaughter's adopted son"—David regarded his grandnephew as blood.

In 1979, Batya was out for Chinese food when she noticed that her food had a metallic flavor to it. When the odd symptom persisted, she went to a doctor who determined that she was bleeding internally. Batya was diagnosed with a rare form of muscle cancer, leiomyosarcoma, that had no established treatment.

After receiving the diagnosis, Batya threw herself into preparing her family for a future without her. She enrolled them all in therapy, though Sol dropped out after the first day. Batya made Rochelle promise that she and Ben would continue with therapy, even after her death.

Batya taught Ben how to manage the billing for Sol's business so that he could take over the task when she grew infirm. She gave Paula specific directions about how she wanted the logistics of her funeral to proceed, including the meal that followed. Though the two had their conflicts, Paula was the only person Batya trusted to faithfully execute her wishes.

As Batya grew sicker, the reality of how much Sol relied on her came into focus for him. Unable to cope with the news, let alone care for his terminally ill wife, Sol fell apart. Batya moved in with Rochelle and Norman, and Rochelle quit her job to provide full-time care to Batya for over a year. Ben continued living with his father until graduating from high school and moved out shortly thereafter.

In December 1982, Michael Bakst threw David a sixtieth birthday party. Batya, not wanting to miss her brother's party, showed up shockingly ashen and in a wheelchair. She was unable to stay long, but she made it. She died just days later.

By the time Batya passed away, the Bakst home was nearly empty. The three eldest children were out of college, with David having provided both tuition funds and frequent care packages filled with Mirobe-distributed salamis and cheeses. Rochelle Bakst moved upstate and later to Florida, working as a substance abuse counselor before Steven convinced her to go into business with him. Steven completed four years of college but left before receiving a degree to open his first closeout store with Bernie. He bought into the partnership using money saved from his bar mitzvah, managed the store, and opened multiple others thereafter. After being double crossed by Bernie one too many times, Steven started his own successful franchise company with Rochelle in New York.

Gary and his wife Linda met at Binghamton University and relocated to Pittsburgh for Gary's medical schooling. While Gary almost missed the deadline for applying—he briefly second guessed whether he truly wanted to be a doctor or if the decision was a product of his father's conditioning—he graduated with honors in 1986. David cried through the entire ceremony. At one point he leaned over to Linda. "Who would have thought I would get to see this?" he whispered. "I had nothing when I came here."

As the baby of the family, Doreen had a different childhood from that of her siblings. The house was more spacious, Paula and

David's traumas less fresh, and the family no longer bore the stress of living paycheck to paycheck. Whereas Steven was forced to wear hand-me-down clothes well into high school, David bought Doreen brand new boots for a ski trip with her United Synagogue Youth friends. Doreen never suffered the nightmares that plagued Rochelle well into her thirties, though she still felt the silent responsibility to find success that came with being the child of survivors. A few years later, she followed in Gary's footsteps and earned a biology degree from Binghamton University.

While Doreen was in college, Michael Bakst, debilitated by years of substance abuse, announced that he no longer wished for Mirobe to compensate Tommy and Nicki. He demanded that David cease payments. The decision drove the immensely profitable business into the ground and left Michael sleeping with a gun under his pillow in Saint Croix out of fear that the men might retaliate.

Though David and Paula were financially stable—Paula had been dutifully stashing away portions of David's paychecks for years—losing his livelihood was hard on David. After building a life from scraps and rising to command a booming business, he was suddenly forced into retirement, forfeiting much of the pension that he was promised by Mirobe. The ordinarily cheerful man fell into a depression.

PHOTOS

Lea Silberfarb, Havana, Cuba, July 26, 1956.

Left to right: Paula Bakst holding Steven Bakst, Rochelle Bakst, Lea Silberfarb. New York, early 1957.

Sol Feder and Batya Feder at their wedding in 1959.

Steven Bakst and Leah Silberfarb in New York, late 1950s.

David Bakst holding Gary Bakst with Steven Bakst and Rochelle Bakst at their home in Rosedale, New York, around 1960.

Paula Bakst holding Gary Bakst with Steven Bakst and Rochelle Bakst in New York, around 1960.

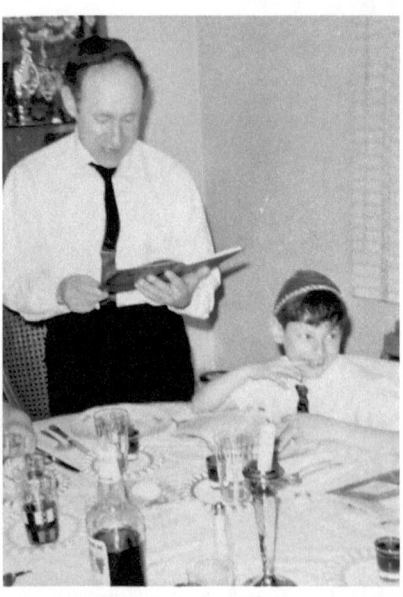

David Bakst leading a holiday meal with Gary Bakst at their home in Rosedale, New York, early to mid-1960s.

Bernie Silberfarb's wedding. Back row, left to right: Marvin Bressler, Lea Silberfarb, Lisa Keitel, Bernie Silberfarb, David Bakst. Front row, left to right: Sophia Bressler, Steven Bakst, Paula Bakst, Rochelle Bakst. New York, early to mid-1960s.

David Bakst in his office at Mirobe, date unknown.

Left to right: Lea Silberfarb and Paula Silberfarb in Paula's kitchen. Date unknown.

Steven Bakst's Bar Mitzvah. Back row, left to right: Rochelle Bakst, Paula Bakst, Lea Silberfarb. Front row: Doreen Bakst. New York, October 1969.

Doreen Bakst's Bat Mitzvah. Left to right: Steven Bakst, Gary Bakst, Rochelle Bakst, David Bakst, Paula Bakst, Doreen Bakst, Sophia Bressler, Marvin Bressler, Stewart Bressler, Muriel Bressler, Abraham Bressler. Long Island, New York, April 27, 1980.

Doreen Bakst's Bat Mitzvah. Back row, left to right: Ben Feder, David Bakst, Norman Stern. Middle row, left to right: Gary Bakst, Steven Bakst, Larry Stern, Sol Feder. Front row, left to right: Rochelle Bakst, Paula Bakst, Doreen Bakst, Batya Feder, Rochelle Stern. Long Island, New York, April 27, 1980.

Doreen's Bat Mitzvah. Back row, left to right: David Bakst, Paula Bakst. Front row, left to right: Bushe Rozen, Nucham Rozen. Long Island, New York, April 27, 1980.

28

In the 1990s, a telephone rang in a condo in Liberty, New York. David answered.

"Are you David Bakszt?" inquired an unfamiliar voice.

David responded affirmatively.

"Your father is Berko Bakszt?"

"Yes, who is this?" David asked, in his characteristically blunt but well-intentioned fashion.

The woman on the other end of the line began to weep. She explained through tears that her father was among the Jews whom Berko had fed and smuggled out of the Iwje ghetto through his leathermaking factory in the early 1940s. The woman's father had managed to survive the war and eventually made his way to Canada. "I'm alive because of your father," the caller said to David with gratitude.

David and Paula relocated to the Inner Circle, a townhouse community developed by the Brown's Hotel in the Catskills. David, *kvelling* over the birth of his four grandchildren, eventually rebounded from his depression and became a hotshot in the community. He served as vice president of the condominium board, led daily prayer services in the neighborhood clubhouse, and resolved the challenges that plagued the upstate community, such as persuading the town to plow their private roads in the wintertime.

The couple regularly attended Shabbat services at a nearby temple, their faith never shaken, and frequently entertained neighbors who became close friends. Paula continued cooking and baking, hosting the extended family for every Jewish holiday and still making her gefilte fish from scratch each Passover.

After so many years, Paula and David remained happily married. Though he was more of a strawberry shortcake fan, David habitually requested chocolate birthday cakes because they were Paula's favorite. Taped to the dashboard of their Lincoln was a note in Paula's distinctive cursive handwriting: *"Put on your seatbelt. I love you."*

To the best of the Bakst family's knowledge, only three people involved in the deaths of Paula and David's relatives ever faced criminal charges. The paths to justice were lengthy and often unfulfilling.

On December 15, 1966, the Germans indicted Leopold Windisch and Rudolf Werner for war crimes. The men were charged with conducting a series of disturbingly similar mass executions in Lida, Zoludek, Vasiliski, Voronovo, and Iwje over the course of five days. The German authorities attributed approximately 13,000 deaths to Windisch and Werner's actions.[1] That figure includes the thousands of Jews shot on May 12, 1942, in Iwje during the selection that the Bakszt family was forced to attend.

Windisch became a member of the Hitler youth at age fourteen in Austria, eventually relocating to Germany and joining the *Sturmabteilung* (the SA or Nazi Party's paramilitary wing).[2] He was alleged to have supervised the marketplace selection and covering of the mass grave in Iwje and to have managed *aktionen* in several other towns.[3]

Werner joined the Nazi Party in 1937.[4] The prosecutors accused Werner of participating in the same mass executions as Windisch had and shooting several Jews.[5] Werner claimed "politically innocent" status in post-war paperwork, attempting to evade authorities.[6]

Between the late 1940s and mid-1960s, the Austrians opened and closed several cases against Windisch, determining each time that the prosecutors lacked jurisdiction to proceed against a noncitizen for crimes occurring outside Austria's borders.[7] The Germans' first attempt at trying cases against Windisch and Werner in 1968 ended in a mistrial, when a *Mainz Landgericht* (Mainz district court) official secretly wiretapped the proceeding.[8] The state prosecutor thereafter dropped the charges against Werner, determining that he was unfit to stand trial due to diabetes and arteriosclerosis.[9] Werner died in 1971.[10]

Windisch was retried in 1969 and ultimately convicted on July 17, 1969, in a 136-page verdict.[11] He was found guilty of facilitating mass murders in Lida, Zoludek, Vasilishki, Voronovo, and Iwje on May 8 through 12, 1942.[12] Windisch was acquitted on other murder charges.[13] He was sentenced to life in prison, stripped of his German citizenship, and ultimately died in 1985 after a failed appeal.[14]

Ivan Polyukhovich was a Ukrainian man who was born in Serniki in 1916 and lived in a neighboring village.[15] When the Nazis invaded, they equipped Polyukhovich with weapons and, as with many local forest wardens at the time, tasked him with locating fugitives in the woods surrounding Serniki.[16] After the war, Polyukhovich hid among refugees in a displaced persons camp in Fallingbostel, Germany, and obtained an Australian visa.[17]

Polyukhovich lived an ordinary life in Adelaide, Australia, for decades.[18] He worked as a farm laborer and public servant and gifted neighbors honey harvested from the bees he raised behind his suburban bungalow.[19] But when Polyukhovich's stepdaughters returned to Ukraine to visit relatives in the 1980s, word spread that the infamous man was alive and well.[20] Suddenly, Ukrainian locals and the Soviet Union were lobbying Australian authorities to prosecute Polyukhovich, alleging that he was responsible for the deaths of hundreds of Serniki Jews and Soviet partisans.[21]

The reports fomented an extensive investigation. An eyewitness placed Polyukhovich at the scene of the 1942 mass killing in Serniki, during which Polyukhovich allegedly ushered the Jews to the pit, gun in hand.²² That witness—who at sixteen years old was forced by the Germans to cover the mass grave—led an Australian forensic team into the woods, adamant that an otherwise unremarkable area of the forest was in fact the unmarked burial site.²³

In a joint operation with the Soviets, the Australians discovered that they were indeed standing atop a fifty-meter-long by ten-meter-wide gravesite, filled with layers of densely packed skeletons.²⁴ Analysis of soil disturbances revealed that the Nazis had dug a forty-five degree entry ramp on the eastern side of the pit, likely used to march the victims into the grave before they were shot.²⁵ Examining the top layer of bodies alone, the excavators found 553 sets of human remains, many still surrounded by Jewish prayer shawls and yarmulkes.²⁶ Bullet holes, shot haphazardly, pierced countless of the skulls, with bullets and cartridge casings strewn beside the bodies.²⁷

The excavation and forensic evidence corroborated eyewitness accounts of Polyukohvich's participation. Consistent with testimony that Polyukohvich and two other men had forced a woman and two children into the grave after the killings, excavators found the remains of a mother, with a young child next to her and the bones of an infant still in her arms, lying at a higher elevation than the other skeletons.²⁸

In January 1990, Australians charged Polyukhovich with participating in the mass execution of 850 Jews from the Serniki ghetto, among other murder counts.²⁹ After a protracted legal battle in which the Australian Supreme Court reversed the magistrate judge's partial summary dismissal, a jury found Polyukohvich not guilty on all charges.³⁰ As in the failed Australian trials of two other alleged Nazi collaborators, the prosecution could not definitively prove that Polyukhovich himself had fired any of the bullets found in the Serniki grave.³¹ Much of Paula's extended family is buried in that mass grave.

David and Paula remained strong supporters of Holocaust education. The couple contributed to the United States Holocaust Memorial Museum's establishment and attended its 1993 dedication ceremonies. They frequently shared their stories with family and inquisitive friends. David was a regular speaker at annual Iwje Society meetings and Holocaust Remembrance Day events, moving crowds with his ability to vividly describe the pain and pride of being a survivor. Unlike many other Jews who escaped Nazi Europe to be burdened by a lifetime of trauma, David managed to find happiness and often focused his speeches on Jewish resistance and resurrection from tragedy. He was an outspoken Zionist, viewing Israel not only as the birthplace of his Jewish heritage but also as the sole place where Jews were safe from future persecution. In a 1989 *Yom HaShoah* service, David shared the following excerpted remarks:

> *Z'chor, Gedenk, Remember. That is why we have gathered here to remember the Holocaust. The horror and death that took the lives of six million European Jews and destroyed their religious and cultural institutions. A Holocaust doesn't just happen. It is a deliberate calculated act of mass murder in which the murderers are not only those who do the killing, but those who stand by and do nothing to stop it. We must recognize the early symptoms of this hideous disease. The early symptoms of Nazi evil were always there. Hitler made it very clear in Mein Kampf published in 1925. In 1933, as Chancellor of Germany, he began to terrorize the Jews. In 1935, the Nuremberg Laws turned Jews into non-people. On the infamous Kristallnacht, 191 synagogues were burned to the ground. There was nothing secret about these atrocities. American diplomats sent detailed reports to the State Department of what they had seen. The whole world knew — and did nothing.*
>
> *We remember, in May 1939, a luxury liner called the St. Louis sailed from Germany with 930 Jews to Cuba. But the Cuban government would not allow them to land, and neither would the American government. Thinking there might be a change of heart in Washington, the captain of the St. Louis drifted off the coast of Florida, close enough for the passengers to see the lights of Miami. But the Americans' only response to this crisis was to dispatch a coast guard vessel to shadow the St. Louis to make certain that none of the passengers tried to enter*

Florida by swimming. The ship returned to Germany. The world knew —and the world did nothing.

Today, for you and me and for all of us it is not too late. We will remain vigilant, ever alert to the fires of antisemitism. It is our obligation to remember; to remember is a duty, a personal duty and we must not only remember how it ended, but also how it began. The cherished dream our six million did not live to see is becoming a reality. Remembrance must make us all better human beings with more love for our people and our heritage. Memory is pain, but also our treasure, the source of our strength. To remember the Holocaust is our mission in life. It adds a special dimension to Jewish unity and solidarity. Preserving this memory is the sacred duty of all of us who care for a better future for the Jewish people, for Israel, and for all mankind.

If we survived Hitler, it is only because of our spiritual strength. Our faith which emerged with dignity from the ashes of Treblinka and the mass graves of Bergen-Belsen and Babi Yar; from the partisans, from the forest, from the hiding places, from the bunkers and from each shtetl in Europe. The survivors harbored in their lives not only the grief of their own losses, but also a deep Jewish pride which they carried along with fruitful vitality and dynamism. Wherever they built new homes, in Israel, in America, and all other countries, they reestablished families, raised children, they became useful, productive members of society with notable and significant contributions in all walks of life. Indeed, they sanctified life by rebuilding it from the ashes. They became a moral force in the communities where they dwell with their experiences and achievements.

From the great catastrophe that destroyed a third of our people, we carried the torch of remembrance which lit up our souls and has kindled the flame of life and rebirth, personal and national. Those who love freedom, those who battle against oppression and bigotry draw strength from our victory. We walked through the fire and survived. Our survival is the next and future generations' survival.

In the mid-1990s, Sol and Ben Feder visited Sol's hometown of Frampol, Poland. The village looked as though it had been frozen in time; the rickety wooden barn in which Sol had hid naked from the Nazis was still standing. Sol, eager to show Ben his childhood home, had a local guide knock on the door. The current owner took one look at the men and shouted at them in Polish, "Get out from here, or I'll throw you out!"

Some locals had learned to mask their antisemitism more effectively. As he walked through the streets of Frampol, Sol noticed a man gesturing excitedly at him. Over the span of several seconds, Sol's facial expression transitioned from confusion to horror to rage as he realized that the man waiving at him was the same man who had thrown rocks through the grate as Sol hid in a sewer drain from the Nazis. In a rather apparent act of karma, the man had since somehow lost his right arm.

Other towns have addressed their histories with greater sensitivity. When David's friend, Allen Small, returned to Iwje, he found it devoid of Jewish life but conscious of its past. The town erected a memorial where the mass executions had occurred and holds a yearly ceremony to commemorate the liquidation of the Iwje ghetto.

David and Moshe Baran remained lifelong friends, even after Moshe eventually relocated to Pittsburgh. In 1999, shortly after Doreen's wedding, Moshe sent the following letter to David:

> *I would like to tell you again how happy we were to be present at your simhah! Hearing the name Bakst repeated several times, my memory flashed back to a time long ago to the ghetto Krasny in the year 1943. A place where thousands of Jews from the annihilated schtetlech have been trapped, hopeless, despondent, starved and sick. We were among them. I do not remember the details, but unexpectedly someone found our family and delivered a package of food, sent by your father.*
>
> *Dear David, neither I, nor my family, met your father before the war. (I was told by my mother that your mother was related to her.) I am at a loss for words to describe what it meant in those horror-filled days to receive food, to know that someone cared! Your father, although himself in danger, managed to find a gentile who dared to undertake this mission.*
>
> *I met your father for the first time after the war and found him to be*

a kind and caring person. I understand what moved him to do what he did for us and probably for others as well. When he found out that part of our family survived he insisted that we move from the barracks of a temporary displaced persons camp and join his family who found more comfortable housing in Braunau.

I want to share these memories with your children and grandchildren so that they will know and appreciate the wonderful qualities of their grandparents even more.

At one hundred years old, Moshe remains a strong advocate of Holocaust education. On the morning of Saturday, October 27, 2018, the sound of gunshots pierced his neighborhood. Moshe lives mere blocks from the Tree of Life Synagogue and was attending Shabbat services at another nearby temple that was sent into lockdown. A gunman entered the Tree of Life Synagogue, shouted "all Jews must die," and opened fired on the worshipping congregants.[32] Armed with an AR-15-style assault rifle and multiple handguns, the terrorist killed eleven Jews and wounded six others.[33]

In the hours and weeks before the attack, the gunman posted antisemitic and xenophobic rants online about HIAS,[34] the same organization that had arranged the Silberfarbs' transit to Cuba and helped 134 of the displaced persons on David's ship come to America.[35] HIAS has resettled more than 4.5 million people in effectuating its mission of advocating for refugees and asylum seekers across the globe.[36] Though the organization historically partnered with the State Department on refugee resettlement,[37] the relationship devolved during the Trump Administration. HIAS condemned many of President Trump's attempted changes to American immigration policy, including implementing historically low refugee resettlement quotas[38] and dismantling asylum protections.[39] It sued the Administration over its travel ban on Muslim refugees.[40] The clash garnered the ire of right-wing extremists, including the Tree of Life gunman. The shooting was the deadliest attack on a Jewish community in the United States.[41]

A few years earlier, the American Society for Yad Vashem hosted its inaugural Florida Tribute Dinner at a synagogue in Boca

Raton. The event honored Aron Bell—formerly Aron Bielski—the last surviving Bielski brother.[42] It was well attended, populated by dignitaries, a senator, and survivors and their descendants.[43] Among the nearly 300-person crowd[44] were Gary and David Bakst and Gary's friend Warren Geisler along with his United States-army-veteran father, Morty Geisler.

Gary and Warren arranged for the four of them to share dinner. It was a particularly meaningful opportunity for David, whose group of still-living friends and fellow survivors had dwindled substantially. David and Morty swapped stories of their time in the Allied Forces as their sons listened on in awe. The elderly men quickly bonded, identifying with one another in a way that only those who had experienced early-1940s Europe could.

David began reflecting on his final days as a Soviet soldier in Magdeburg, Germany, recounting how he initially mistook the American forces for the enemy. Morty interjected, explaining that he was one of the American soldiers who had entered Magdeburg on tanks that day. Sitting at a table in America with their children more than seventy years later, the two men recalled celebrating the end of World War II together.

EPILOGUE

By the time their four grandchildren arrived, Paula and David—or Bubby and Poppy as they are more affectionately known—had softened. It wasn't until I was well into grade school that I noticed that their near-perfect English was delivered through Eastern European accents. The Hebrew day school my brother and I attended had an annual grandparents' day. When I was in kindergarten, my teacher sympathetically pulled me aside to explain that my grandparents called to say that they were having car trouble and would not be able to make it. I looked at her incredulously, "No, they'll be here." Though delayed and driving a rental car, Bubby and Poppy made the two-hour drive to grandparents' day that year. They made it every subsequent year too, a grand total of eleven times, until both my brother and I graduated.

Growing up, Bubby and Poppy were frequently around. When my mother returned to work after her maternity leave, they watched me several days a week, considering it a favor bestowed upon them. Insistent that his infant granddaughter promptly meet all development milestones, Poppy spent those days holding me under my arms and walking me around the house. To his sheer delight—and likely due to his intervention—I was walking by eight months old. When my brother was young, Poppy spent hours playing with him on the floor, never once suggesting that the position might be uncomfortable for the then-near octogenarian. My happiest childhood memories remain the spring days when Bubby and Poppy returned to the East Coast for the summer, and I sprinted up the driveway from the school bus to greet them.

When I was three, my parents pulled a miserable me out of nursery school. That afternoon I exclaimed, "Poppy, I don't have to go to school anymore!" As a man who prized education, he looked at me with dismay. "What do you mean? You can't drop out of school!" While his stubborn meddling may have frustrated my parents, I held my own against him. His response was that I would be a lawyer one day (though he continued to remind me that "there's nothing wrong with being a doctor" until I actually took the Law School Admission Test two decades later).

Poppy was not one to shy away from the limelight. He taught himself to play the mandolin by ear and sang along in Yiddish. Poppy was a talented and spry performer with a dulcet voice. He starred in several local musical theater productions, including as Tevye in Fiddler on the Roof. Even when Poppy, an unwaveringly loyal husband, was well into his eighties, Bubby continued to get jealous of the women who played his love interests in his community shows and concerts.

Bubby and Poppy bought a condominium in Florida to escape the New York winters. Down South, Poppy became *gabbi* and a board member of the Century Village temple in Pembroke Pines. He attended prayer services every morning, often leading the congregation. Poppy *davened* (prayed) with gut-wrenching emotion. As one of his fellow congregants described, "When David *davens* he takes me back to the great days of Europe and the Lower East Side of Manhattan. He brings tears to my eyes!" His rabbi echoed the sentiment. Fifteen years later, people still remark to me how Poppy so passionately led the *Musaf* prayer service at my bat mitzvah.

While Poppy was certainly a product of his generation, he also embraced modernity. It was important to him that his grandchildren—women and men alike—grew up to be self-sufficient. He remained curious about pop culture, even asking about Lady Gaga after hearing one of her songs on the radio. One Shabbat morning, my brother and I attended services with Bubby and Poppy at their synagogue in Liberty, New York. When the rabbi offered my brother an *aliyah*, I told my grandfather that I wanted one too. Poppy insisted that his granddaughter be allowed to have the same honor. To everyone's astonishment, he managed to persuade the Orthodox rabbi to make an exception to the synagogue's male-only rule. I got my *aliyah*.

Bubby is more reserved. Her reticence can be mistaken for standoffishness, but she is deeply sweet once she warms to you. She showed her love by feeding us, always having matzo ball soup and sponge cake waiting. If my brother did not eat enough to her liking, she would patiently feed him bite by bite, pretending each forkful was a train approaching the station; this lasted well beyond the point at which Jordan was capable of feeding himself.

Bubby spent countless hours teaching me how to play Rummikub, crochet, and bake her unrivaled almond cookies. Having learned to sew during the war, she was an expert seamstress, a blessing given that my mother could never find pants that properly fit my lanky figure or my brother's non-existent waist. We lugged over garbage bags filled with clothes, which she precisely and promptly altered. Thanks to Bubby, she and Poppy were also always immaculately dressed; typically, him in a collared shirt, slacks, and suspenders, and her in a suit.

Bubby's unassuming nature masked her brilliance. She spoke six languages to varying degrees—English, Hebrew, Yiddish, Polish, Russian, and Spanish—and often helped me with my Hebrew and math homework as a child. Her quiet but methodical approach kept the household running, from directing Poppy's driving to preventing him from overstepping with a gentle squeeze of the forearm. (Occasionally, her warnings came too late. In such cases, Poppy was usually ordered back to apologize the next day.) Bubby also meticulously accounted for every penny earned and spent on a handwritten ledger. When Gary started medical school, it was

Bubby who handed his wife the literal wad of cash to deliver to the bursar's office.

The walls of Bubby and Poppy's apartment are plastered with heirlooms from Israel, Batya's paintings, and pictures of family spanning the generations from their grandparents to their great-granddaughter. Among the prints from countless bar and bat mitzvahs, weddings, and school picture days are three striking images. Above a giant black-and-white photograph of Bubby and Poppy at their wedding in Cuba sit matching paintings of Berko and Rochel Bakszt. Though Rochel's face is clear, the perimeter of the portrait remains unfinished; Batya died before completing it. The third is a picture of me standing next to my great-grandfather Berko's grave in Hofgeismar. The photo is nearly identical to one Poppy took in the same spot sixty-five years earlier. I was the first family member to have returned since Poppy fled Europe. While there are no longer Jews living in Hofgeismar, local officials continue to maintain the Jewish cemetery and a nearby Jewish museum used to teach local schoolchildren about the Holocaust. After my trip, Poppy told my father that he had been anxious for decades about the state of his father's grave. "Now, I can die in peace," Poppy said.

Though one would not have known it by looking at him, Poppy's medical chart was enough to shock any doctor: lung cancer, kidney disease, hypertension, years of chronic atrial fibrillation, diabetes, and congestive heart failure. Until his nineties, he walked on the treadmill daily and did push-ups each morning, maintaining an impressive set of biceps. As his health began to decline, Poppy almost never complained, even when he received monthly shots directly into his eyes for macular degeneration. Having never expected to live beyond his twentieth birthday, Poppy viewed each day as a gift.

Poppy passed away peacefully from natural causes on December 22, 2020—thirty-eight years after his sister Batya's death to the exact day. That he lived to ninety-eight with such a normal quality of life was itself a miracle and a testament to his grit; during his final few years Poppy was hospitalized on numerous occasions with discouraging prognoses, only to miraculously recover each time. It was also a testament to his son Dr. Gary Bakst's sound medical advice and unrelenting advocacy.

In the aftermath of Poppy's passing, I have been astounded by the number of lives that he enriched. Though he had not lived in the area for a few years, multiple former congregants from his defunct upstate New York synagogue attended his graveside funeral in masks and winter gear due to the COVID-19 pandemic. The Inner Circle's long-time landscaper pulled my mother aside to tell her how Poppy once prevented the community board from accepting another company's cheaper bid by insisting that the man's years of reliable service justified his contract renewal. Poppy's children were flooded with calls and cards from Poppy's former rabbis, friends in Florida, fellow congregants, and far-extended family who shared loving memories of visits with Poppy. Even my father's former bookkeeper recalled that when Poppy had visited his children's business and learned that she had no grandparents, he offered to be her grandfather.

Bubby, now ninety, is too ravaged by Alzheimer's to know who I am but still lights up with joy when I visit and insists that she hold my hand. In earlier stages of the disease when her long-term memory remained intact, she often reverted to memories of her childhood in Serniki, asking about her mother's whereabouts and confusing her son Steven for her brother, Bernie. Over a cup of tea, Bubby once mentioned to her daughter-in-law that she was concerned about her father. "I worry that he was buried alive," she said, unprompted.[1]

Though she has lost most of her faculties, Bubby somehow still recognized Poppy, and often Poppy only. Despite her compromised memory and aphasia, Bubby shocked everyone when she repeatedly asked about Poppy's whereabouts in the weeks after his death. They were happily married for over seventy years.

And as Bubby and Poppy would say, their children and grandchildren brought them "only *nachas*." In cleaning out their apartment, our family found countless mementos that they saved over the years: old articles about my father's business successes;

middle school essays I wrote about them and their families; and a folded-up paper in Poppy's wallet scrawled with his grandchildren's then-schooling: "Laura at Harvard Law School. Jordan Cornell." (Though Poppy was eager to boast, he was forgetful.)

Gary and his wife Linda have two children: Daniel, married to Beth, works in real estate asset management and gave Bubby and Poppy their first great-grandchild, Evelyn; and Leah, married to Ben, is a neuroscience PhD and talented musician. In addition to monitoring Bubby's medical care, including ensuring she received medication that significantly slowed the progression of her disease, Gary continues to help patients as an endocrinologist in Albany, New York. Linda, a talented writer, has documented much of her in-laws' stories.

Steven and his wife Shari—a retired director for New York State's Office for People with Developmental Disabilities—also have two children. Jordan, my younger brother, followed me to law school and is an associate at a law firm in Manhattan. I spent the last two years clerking in the same New York City federal courthouse where my grandparents became United States citizens over sixty-five years ago. Taking after my namesake Batya, I hope to use my legal degree to advance reproductive rights and gender equality.

My father, Steven, followed in his uncle's footsteps and started a successful business in his twenties. He and his sister Rochelle ran a dollar-store franchise company, Just-A-Buck, and partnered with nonprofit franchisees that hire and train people with disabilities at the stores. They also employed Bubby and Poppy for years as the couple learned to cope with their empty nest and the downfall of Mirobe. In retirement, Steven hones his mechanical skills, constantly working on projects around the house and repairing his family's broken appliances. Rochelle is generous with her time and coordinates Bubby's care needs and insurance paperwork.

Doreen continues to work in corporate management for Just-A-Buck and handles Bubby and Poppy's finances. She is married to Darren Fleischman, a history teacher, and lives near Rochelle Bakst outside of Kingston, New York.

Sophia and Bernie passed away in 2018 and 2020, respectively. Both suffered from dementia. Sophia had a challenging life. She eventually left Marvin after several decades of abuse, though their relationship remained cordial until his death. They lost their daughter, Muriel, in 2001. Sophia spent her elderly years in Arizona near her two sons and two granddaughters, writing poems and short stories about her life in Serniki. Albeit under pressure from Poppy, Bernie continued to financially support Sophia until her last day. Bernie amassed substantial wealth as a businessman before retiring to Florida, leaving the business to one of his two sons. Each has three children.

Uncle Nucham lived well into his nineties and left behind his own generations of descendants. He maintained a lifelong relationship with Bubby and is regarded by her children as a pure *mensch*. Sol Feder, now ninety-six, resides in Florida. He is widowed a second time and cared for by Rochelle Stern and Ben. Rochelle divorced Norman and became a nurse anesthetist. Her home is decorated with Batya's sketches and paintings. Ben, a lawyer, has two sons in college, neither of whom Batya lived long enough to meet. The youngest is named after Ilana, the baby Batya tried to save in the Nazi work camp. To this day, Ben still has the Torah that his mother rescued from the woods in Poland.

The second- and third-generation Baksts have become more secular, though we remain tied to our Jewish heritage. I can remember my dad singing to me in Yiddish as a kid, the same lullabies his Bubby Lea sang to him. When we were building our house, Poppy brought us silver dollars dated 1971—the numbers adding up to eighteen, or *chai*. Like Poppy's father had done with him in Iwje, Poppy and my father had my brother and me press the coins into the just-poured concrete corners of the foundation. After Bubby grew too old to host Passover seders, Steven did, making gefilte fish from scratch using his mother's recipe and three different types of fish. (Thankfully, he did not employ our bathtub in the process.)

In 1994, Steven Spielberg founded the Shoah Foundation to conduct and preserve interviews with Holocaust survivors. As we rapidly approach the day that first-hand witnesses will no longer be with us, the Institute has amassed more than 55,000 testimonies from sixty-five countries in forty-three languages.[2] Both Bubby and Poppy recorded testimonies in 1995. Bubby's ends with her surrounded by the family she created: Poppy, their four children, two daughters-in-law, and four grandchildren. Her children reflect on the substantial second-hand effects that the Holocaust has had on them, followed by Poppy playing a Hebrew song about the promise of the future on the mandolin as then-two-year-old me happily dances around.[3] Poppy concluded his own testimony with the following comments, while choking back tears:

> *I am the one that has the opportunity from a whole town, and at times I felt that I am the representative of my shtetl, that I speak for everybody. . . . I always think that [Jews] should be proud of what we are and we should speak out against antisemites . . . . We have a glorious history, that's what my father used to tell me always, we have a glorious history, we should be very proud. . . .*
>
> *I have sleepless nights. I'm nervous sometimes. But I . . . always say to myself, look what you accomplished. You have a family. After me I left a generation, and I have grandchildren. Not everybody had the opportunity. Not everybody was privileged to have that. I have it. And that's what gives me life. Because, my life is just like my father, family comes first. That's the most important to me in my life right now. . . .*
>
> *I am happy. If there is a prayer that I could say, and I'm sure there is a prayer in Hebrew that I could say, that I lived to tell this story, I would say that prayer. But I will say in English that I thank God that he gave me the opportunity and I lived to tell this story, that I lived through it.*[4]

BAKST FAMILY TREE

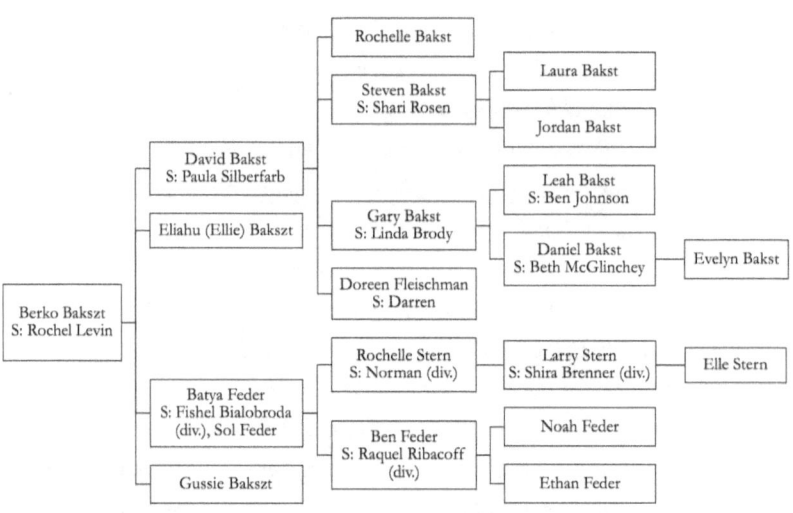

SILBERFARB FAMILY TREE

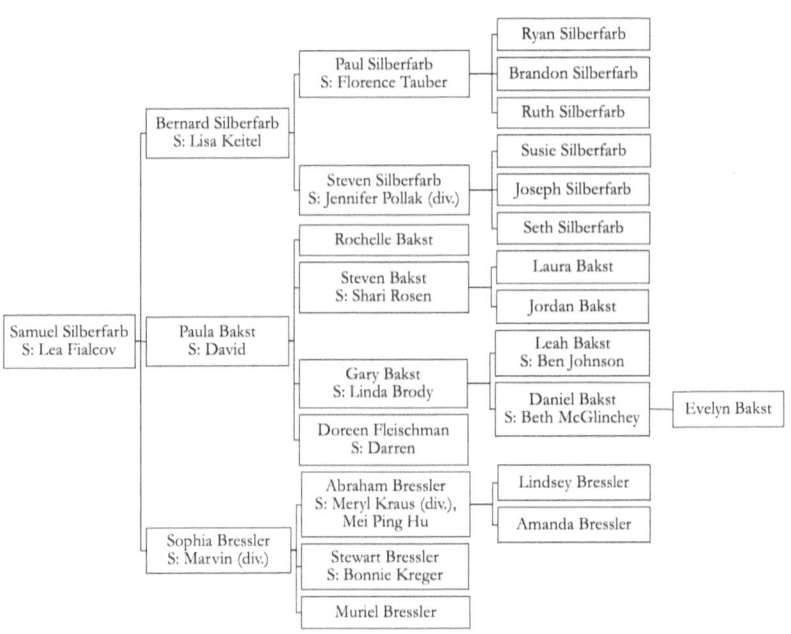

PHOTOS

The Bakst family after Paula Bakst and David Bakst recorded their testimonies for the USC Shoah Foundation. Back row, left to right: Shari Bakst holding Jordan Bakst, Doreen Bakst, Rochelle Bakst, Linda Bakst. Front row, left to right: Steven Bakst holding Laura Bakst, Paula Bakst, David Bakst holding Leah Bakst, Gary Bakst holding Daniel Bakst. Liberty, New York, August 17, 1995.

Jordan Bakst's Siddur Ceremony at Reuben Gittelman Hebrew Day School. Left to right: Steven Bakst, Shari Bakst, Jordan Bakst, Laura Bakst, Paula Bakst, David Bakst. New City, New York, spring 2002.

David Bakst saying weekday morning prayers with his tefillin and tallit. Florida, date unknown.

Left to right: Ben Feder, Paula Bakst, Sophia Bressler. Location and date unknown.

Laura Bakst's Bat Mitzvah. Left to right: David Bakst, Paula Bakst, Jordan Bakst, Laura Bakst, Steven Bakst, Shari Bakst. Monroe, New York, March 18, 2006.

David Bakst saying the blessing over the challah bread at Laura Bakst's Bat Mitzvah. Left to right: Leah Bakst, Laura Bakst, David Bakst, Jordan Bakst, Daniel Bakst. New City, New York, March 18, 2006.

David Bakst as Tevye in Fiddler on the Roof. Florida, date unknown.

Paula Bakst and David Bakst's 60th anniversary party. Back row, left to right: Daniel Bakst behind his wife, Beth Bakst; Darren Fleischman behind his wife, Doreen Fleischman; Steven Bakst behind his wife, Shari Bakst; Rachel Feder behind her husband, Sol Feder; Rochelle Stern behind Sophia Bressler; Steven (Linda Bakst's brother) next to his wife, Cindy, and behind his mother, Feige; Gary Bakst behind his wife, Linda Bakst, and next to Jordan Bakst. Squatting/sitting, left to right: Laura Bakst, Rochelle Bakst, Paula Bakst, David Bakst, Leah Bakst. Albany, New York, September 2010.

Paula Bakst and David Bakst outside their home in Liberty, New York, after temple services. Date unknown.

Laura Bakst at Berko Bakszt's grave. Hofgeismar, Germany, October 2013.

Left to right: Rochelle Stern, Sol Feder, Ben Feder. New York, 2010s.

Left to right: David Bakst, Paula Bakst, Bernie Silberfarb at Paula and David's condo in Pembroke Pines, Florida, March 2015.

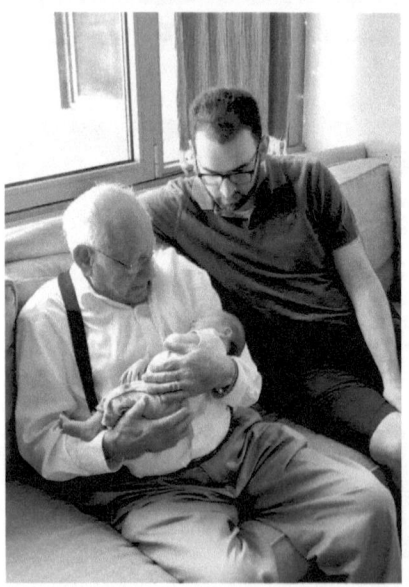

David Bakst, holding his great-granddaughter, Evelyn Bakst, for the first time, with Daniel Bakst. New York, June 2018.

Paula Bakst and David Bakst on their 70th anniversary at their condo in Pembroke Pines, Florida, September 3, 2020.

NOTES

Chapter 1

1. Iwje, also spelled Ivye or Iwie and pronounced ive-yeh, is in modern-day Belarus near the Lithuanian border.
2. Yehuda Leib Bloch, "There Once Was a Shtetl, Ivye," in *In Memory of the Jewish Community of Iwie*, ed. Moshe Kaganowitz, trans. Yocheved Klausner (Tel Aviv: Association of Former Residents of Iwie in Israel, 1968), https://www.jewishgen.org/yizkor/ivye/ivy092.html.
3. Ibid.
4. This translates to "Guaranteed footwear."
5. A *mohel* performs the circumcision during a circumcision ceremony for a newborn male. The *ba'al tekiah* blows the *shofar*, or ram's horn, during *Rosh Hashanah* and *Yom Kippur* services.
6. Avraham Eliav, "Social Activists, House Owners, and Scholars," in *In Memory of the Jewish Community of Iwie*, ed. Moshe Kaganovich (Tel Aviv: Association of Former Residents of Iwie in Israel, 1968), 488.

Chapter 2

1. Located in modern-day northwest Ukraine near the Belarusian border, Serniki is also referred to as Sernyky or Sernik.

Chapter 3

1. "Anti-Jewish Legislation in Prewar Germany," Holocaust Encyclopedia, United States Holocaust Memorial Museum, accessed April 24, 2021, https://encyclopedia.ushmm.org/content/en/article/anti-jewish-legislation-in-prewar-germany.
2. James Q. Whitman, *Hitler's American Model: The United States and the Making of Nazi Race Law* (Princeton: Princeton University Press, 2017), 1–5.
3. "Nuremberg Race Laws," Holocaust Encyclopedia, United States Holocaust Memorial Museum, accessed April 24, 2021, https://encyclopedia.ushmm.org/content/en/article/nuremberg-laws.
4. Ibid.
5. United States Holocaust Memorial Museum, "Anti-Jewish Legislation in Prewar Germany."
6. Ibid.

7. Hannah Arendt, *Eichmann in Jerusalem: A Report on the Banality of Evil* (London: Penguin Books, 2006), 228.

Chapter 4

1. Zeev Barmatz, *Heroism in the Forest: The Jewish Partisans of Belarus* (Tel Aviv: Kotarim International Publishing, 2013), 100.
2. Shifre Margolin, "The Extermination of the Jews in Ivye," in *In Memory of the Jewish Community of Iwie*, ed. Moshe Kaganowitz, trans. Yocheved Klausner (Tel Aviv: Association of Former Residents of Iwie in Israel, 1968), https://www.jewishgen.org/yizkor/ivye/ivy503.html.
3. Ibid.

Chapter 5

1. David Bevan, *A Case to Answer: The Story of Australia's First European War Crimes Prosecution* (Mile End: Wakefield Press, 1994), 2.
2. Ibid.
3. Ibid.
4. Ibid., 3.
5. Ibid.
6. Ibid.

Chapter 6

1. "Iwje," The Untold Stories: The Murder Sites of the Jews in the Occupied Territories of the Former USSR, Yad Vashem, accessed August 20, 2020, https://www.yadvashem.org/untoldstories/database/index.asp?cid=1180.
2. Ibid.
3. Ibid.
4. Margolin, "The Extermination of the Jews in Ivye."
5. Ibid.
6. Ibid.
7. A. Kaplinski, "The Slaughter in Ivye: 12 May 1942-A Day Between Life and Death," in *In Memory of the Jewish Community of Iwie*, ed. Moshe Kaganowitz, trans. Yocheved Klausner (Tel Aviv: Association of Former Residents of Iwie in Israel, 1968), https://www.jewishgen.org/yizkor/ivye/ivy503.html#page519.
8. Barmatz, *Heroism in the Forest*, 101.
9. Kaplinski, "The Slaughter in Ivye: 12 May 1942-A Day Between Life and Death."
10. Ibid.
11. Ibid.
12. Ibid.
13. Ibid.

14. Margolin, "The Extermination of the Jews in Ivye."
15. Kaplinski, "The Slaughter in Ivye: 12 May 1942-A Day Between Life and Death."
16. Ibid.
17. Ibid.
18. Barmatz, *Heroism in the Forest*, 101.
19. Izak Kaplinski, "Testimony of Dr. Izak Kaplinski," JewishGen KehilaLinks, trans. Irene Newhouse, March 25, 1965, https://kehilalinks.jewishgen.org/lida-district/kaplinski.htm.
20. Ibid.
21. Barmatz, *Heroism in the Forest*, 103.
22. Margolin, *The Extermination of the Jews in Ivye*.
23. Ibid.
24. Ibid.
25. Ibid.
26. Ibid.
27. Barmatz, *Heroism in the Forest*, 103.
28. Peter Duffy, *The Bielski Brothers: The True Story of Three Men who Defied the Nazis, Built a Village in the Forest, and Saved 1,200 Jews* (New York: Perennial, 2003), 74.
29. Barmatz, *Heroism in the Forest*, 103.
30. Duffy, *The Bielski Brothers*, 75.

Chapter 7

1. Eliav, "Social Activists, House Owners, and Scholars," 488.
2. Isaac Gordon, interview by Alan Remstein, *Visual History Archive Online*, USC Shoah Foundation, July 17, 1996, Tape 4, 0:30.
3. Barmatz, *Heroism in the Forest*, 103.
4. Gordon, interview, Tape 3, 26:57.
5. Nechama Tec, *Defiance: The Bielski Partisans* (New York: Oxford University Press, 1993), 65.
6. Ibid., 66–67.
7. Ibid., 66.
8. Ibid., 67–68.
9. Ibid., 67.
10. Ibid., 43.
11. "The Bielski Partisans," Holocaust Encyclopedia, United States Holocaust Memorial Museum, accessed August 17, 2020, https://encyclopedia.ushmm.org/content/en/article/the-bielski-partisans.
12. Ibid.
13. Peter Duffy, "Heroes Among Us," *New York Times*, May 28, 2000, https://www.nytimes.com/2000/05/28/nyregion/heroes-among-us.html.
14. "Avnit Makha Kamenetzki," The Central Database of Shoah Victims' Names, Yad Vashem, May 17, 2000, https://yvng.yadvashem.org/nameDetails.html?language=en&itemId=5365820&ind=1.

15. United States Holocaust Memorial Museum, "The Bielski Partisans."
16. Ibid.
17. Ibid.
18. Ibid.
19. David M. Rosen, *Armies of the Young: Child Soldiers in War and Terrorism* (New Brunswick: Rutgers University Press, 2005), 46.
20. Meyshe Kaganovitsh, "From the Great Slaughter to the Liquidation of the Ghetto (12 May 1942 - 20 January 1943)," in *In Memory of the Jewish Community of Iwie*, ed. Moshe Kaganowitz, trans. Yocheved Klausner (Tel Aviv: Association of Former Residents of Iwie in Israel, 1968), https://www.jewishgen.org/yizkor/ivye/ivy525.html#page530; Tec, *Defiance*, 90.
21. M. Kaganovich, ed., "Ivye Natives Who Fell in the Battles Against the Germans," in *In Memory of the Jewish Community of Iwie* (Tel Aviv: Association of Former Residents of Iwie in Israel, 1968), 638.
22. Tec, *Defiance*, 89-90.
23. Ibid., 90.
24. Ibid.
25. Ibid., 90–91.
26. Barmatz, *Heroism in the Forest*, 104.
27. Tec, *Defiance*, 91.
28. Ibid.
29. Ibid.
30. Ibid.
31. Ibid.; Allan Gerald Levine, *Fugitives of the Forest: The Heroic Story of Jewish Resistance and Survival during the Second World War* (Guilford: Lyons Press, 2010), 262.
32. Levine, *Fugitives of the Forest*, 262; Tec, *Defiance*, 91.
33. Tec, *Defiance*, 91.
34. Ibid.
35. Ibid.
36. Ibid.
37. Ibid.
38. Ibid.
39. Ibid.
40. Duffy, *The Bielski Brothers*, 117.
41. Tec, *Defiance*, 91.
42. Ibid.
43. Ibid.; Duffy, *The Bielski Brothers*, 117.
44. Tec, *Defiance*, 91.
45. Ibid.
46. Ibid.
47. Ibid.
48. Ibid., 92.
49. Ibid.
50. Ibid.
51. Ibid.
52. Ibid.

53. Levine, *Fugitives of the Forest*, 263.
54. Ibid.
55. Duffy, *The Bielski Brothers*, 118.
56. The exact story of how Ellie was killed remained unsettled for generations. Historical accounts located in researching this book strongly support the above version of events. The version believed by Ellie's extended family for decades, however, is as follows: Ellie and another partisan were sent to blow up a German train, equipped with explosives and machine guns. They successfully carried out the mission, destroying a Nazi transport and damaging the railway. On the way back to the Bielski camp, the two young men happened upon a farm with a small house nearby. It was late in the day and, overcome with exhaustion, they entered the house with their guns and asked to spend the night. While the Jewish men slept, the owner notified the German authorities. By the time they awoke, the entire house was surrounded by Nazis. The other partisan was shot and killed. Ellie, still holding a machine gun, tried to fire his way out, killing a couple of Germans in the process. He managed to escape the home and run to the fence that surrounded the property. As Ellie was climbing the fence, a Nazi shot him. Ellie collapsed onto the fence and died. Though of little solace, the partisans avenged the deaths. They located the farm and killed the owner who had ratted out the two Jews to the authorities.
57. Duffy, *The Bielski Brothers*, 118.
58. Ibid.

Chapter 8

1. Henning Pieper, *Fegelein's Horsemen and Genocidal Warfare: The SS Cavalry Brigade in the Soviet Union* (Basingstoke: Palgrave Macmillan, 2014), 115.
2. Bevan, *A Case to Answer*, 5.
3. Ibid.

Chapter 9

1. Tec, *Defiance*, 92.
2. Gordon, interview, Tape 4, 16:35.
3. Gordon, interview, Tape 4, 18:46.
4. Gordon, interview, Tape 4, 18:33.
5. Hershel Edelheit and Abraham J. Edelheit, *A World in Turmoil: An Integrated Chronology of the Holocaust and World War II* (Westport: Greenwood Press, 1991), 271.
6. Eliav, "Social Activists, House Owners, and Scholars," 488.
7. Yad Vashem, "Iwje."
8. Gordon, interview, Tape 4, 20:20.
9. Edelheit and Edelheit, *A World in Turmoil*, 271.

Chapter 10

1. "Marvin (Motke) Ginsburg," Jewish Partisan Educational Foundation, accessed September 13, 2020, https://www.jewishpartisancommunity.org/partisans/motke-ginsburg/.
2. Ibid.
3. Ibid.
4. Tec, *Defiance*, 131; J. Jaffe, "Life of Jewish Partisans and Jewish Family Camps in the Forest, From a Diary by a Jewish Partisan, 1942-1943," Yad Vashem, August 12, 1942, https://www.yadvashem.org/docs/life-of-jewish-partisans.html.
5. Tec, *Defiance*, 94–95.
6. Ibid., 95–96.
7. "Holocaust Resistance: Living and Surviving as a Partisan," Jewish Virtual Library, accessed September 13, 2020, https://www.jewishvirtuallibrary.org/living-and-surviving-as-a-partisan.
8. "Partisan Chronicles: Handwritten Partisan Journals" BELTA News Agency and Belarusian State Museum of the Great Patriotic War, accessed September 13, 2020, https://letopis.belta.by/eng/23.

Chapter 12

1. "Lida History," Virtual Shtetl, accessed September 13, 2020, https://sztetl.org.pl/en/towns/l/1071-lida/99-history/137585-history-of-community.
2. Ibid.
3. Yitzchak Rabinowitz, "In the Lida Ghetto," in *The Book of Lida*, eds. Alexander Manor, Itzchak Ganusovitch, and Aba Lando, trans. Roslyn Sherman Greenberg (Tel-Aviv: Former Residents of Lida in Israel and the Committee of Lida Jews in USA, 1970), https://www.jewishgen.org/yizkor/lida/lid288.html#Page301.
4. Jewish Virtual Library, "Holocaust Resistance: Living and Surviving as a Partisan."
5. BELTA News Agency and The Belarusian State Museum of the Great Patriotic War, "Partisan Chronicles: Handwritten Partisan Journals."

Chapter 13

1. Lasitsk is in modern-day southern Belarus near the Ukrainian border.

Chapter 14

1. Fishel Bialobroda, "Between Life and Death," in *The Book of Lida*, eds. Alexander Manor, Itzchak Ganusovitch, and Aba Lando (Tel-Aviv: Former

Residents of Lida in Israel and the Committee of Lida Jews in USA, 1970), 303–04.
2. The specific role Fishel played in Batya's rescue is unknown.
3. "Partisan Hideout," Jewish Partisan Educational Foundation, accessed April 27, 2021, http://www.jewishpartisans.org/hideout.
4. Ibid.
5. Family members have different accounts of Batya's Torah. The recited story is based on David's version. Batya's descendants believe that Batya found the Torah with Fishel in a burning synagogue.

Chapter 15

1. "Matatiahu Bobrov," The Central Database of Shoah Victims' Names, Yad Vashem, May 17, 2000, https://yvng.yadvashem.org/index.html?language=en&s_id=&s_lastName=Bobrov&s_firstName=Matatiahu&s_place=&s_dateOfBirth=&cluster=true.

Chapter 16

1. Krishna Ignalaga Thomas, "Politics of History and Memory: The Russian Rape of Germany in Berlin, 1945," *Historia* 16 (2007): 229–30.
2. Craig W.H. Luther, *The First Day on the Eastern Front: Germany Invades the Soviet Union, June 22, 1941* (Guilford: Stackpole Books, 2018), 66–67.
3. Ibid., 67.
4. Moshe Baran, "Baran, Family Revisit His Shoa Roots in Personal Journey," *Pittsburgh Jewish Chronicle*, September 15, 2010, https://jewishchronicle.timesofisrael.com/baran-family-revisit-his-shoa-roots-in-personal-journey/.
5. Ibid.
6. Moshe Baran, interview by Shulamit Bastacky, *Visual History Archive Online*, USC Shoah Foundation, January 6, 1997, Tape 3, 13:55.
7. Baran, "Baran, Family Revisit His Shoa Roots in Personal Journey;" Baran, interview, Tape 3, 10:50.
8. Baran, interview, Tape 3, 15:07.
9. Baran, interview, Tape 3, 26:00.

Chapter 17

1. Michael Fry, "#tbt: Danzig and the Beginnings of World War II," National Geographic, August 28, 2014, https://blog.education.nationalgeographic.org/2014/08/28/tbt-danzig-and-the-beginnings-of-world-war-ii/.
2. Ibid.
3. Ibid.
4. "Stutthof," Holocaust Encyclopedia, United States Holocaust Memorial Museum, accessed September 13, 2020, https://encyclopedia.ushmm.org/con-

tent/en/article/stutthof.

Chapter 18

1. "Displaced Persons Camps," Yad Vashem, accessed September 13, 2020, https://www.yadvashem.org/articles/general/displaced-persons-camps.html.
2. "The Return to Life in the Displaced Persons Camps, 1945-1956: A Visual Retrospective," Yad Vashem, accessed September 13, 2020, https://www.yadvashem.org/yv/en/exhibitions/dp_ccamp/index.asp; Hart N. Hasten, *I Shall Not Die!* (Jerusalem: Gefen Publishing House, 2003), 44–45.
3. "Displaced Persons," Holocaust Encyclopedia, United States Holocaust Memorial Museum, accessed August 17, 2020, https://encyclopedia.ushmm.org/content/en/article/displaced-persons; William Hageman, "Memories of Displaced Persons Find a Home," *Chicago Tribune*, November 16, 2011, https://www.chicagotribune.com/entertainment/ct-xpm-2011-11-16-ct-ent-1117-museums-ukranian-20111116-story.html.

Chapter 19

1. League of Nations, "The Palestine Mandate," July 24, 1922, Art. 2.
2. Sami Adwan, Dan Bar-On, and Eyal Naveh Prime, eds., *Side by Side: Parallel Histories of Israel-Palestine* (New York: The New Press, 2012), 36, 66, 68.
3. Ibid., 84.
4. Ibid., 96.
5. Ibid., 102.
6. Thomas Albrich and Ronald W. Zweig, eds., *Escape through Austria: Jewish Refugees and the Austrian Route to Palestine* (London: Frank Cass, 2002), 34.
7. Baran, interview, Tape 4, 11:05, 13:37.
8. Albrich and Zweig, *Escape Through Austria*, 25.
9. Ibid., 26–27; Baran, interview, Tape 4, 14:30.
10. Albrich and Zweig, *Escape Through Austria*, 25.
11. Suzanne D. Rutland, "The Transformation of a Community," Israel & Judaism Studies, 2006, https://www.ijs.org.au/jewish-immigration-after-the-second-world-war/; "Postwar Refugee Crisis and the Establishment of the State of Israel," Holocaust Encyclopedia, United States Holocaust Memorial Museum, accessed September 13, 2020, https://encyclopedia.ushmm.org/content/en/article/postwar-refugee-crisis-and-the-establishment-of-the-state-of-israel.
12. Erica S. Goldman-Brodie, ed., "HOF Jewish D.P. Camp," in *The Mass Migration: Jews Leave Eastern Europe*, accessed April 27, 2021, https://www.jewishgen.org/Yizkor/MassMigration/mas054.html.
13. Ibid.
14. Ibid.
15. Ibid.

Chapter 20

1. "Synopsis of Palmach History," Palmach Association, accessed April 30, 2021, https://palmach.org.il/en/history/about/.
2. "Palmach and Illegal Immigration Operations," Palmach Association, accessed April 30, 2021, http://palmach.org.il/en/history/database/?itemId=5028.
3. Mark A. Tessler, *A History of the Israeli-Palestinian Conflict*, 2nd ed. (Bloomington: Indiana University Press, 2009), 256.
4. "Guardian — Herzl," Palmach Association, accessed April 30, 2021, https://palmach.org.il/en/history/database/?itemId=5067.
5. Palmach Association, "Guardian — Herzl"; "The Voyage of the 'Theodor Herzl,'" Palyam.org, accessed April 30, 2021, http://www.palyam.org/English/Hahapala/hf/hf_Theodor_Herzl.pdf.
6. Palmach Association, "Guardian — Herzl"; Palyam.org, "The Voyage of the 'Theodor Herzl.'"
7. Palmach Association, "Guardian — Herzl"; Palyam.org, "The Voyage of the 'Theodor Herzl.'"
8. Palmach Association, "Guardian — Herzl."
9. Ibid.
10. Ibid.
11. Ibid.
12. Ibid.
13. Ibid.
14. Ibid.
15. Ibid.
16. Ibid.
17. Ibid.
18. Ibid.
19. Ibid.
20. Ibid.
21. Ibid.
22. Ibid.
23. Ibid.; Palyam.org, "The Voyage of the 'Theodor Herzl.'"
24. Palmach Association, "Guardian — Herzl."
25. Ibid.
26. Palyam.org, "The Voyage of the 'Theodor Herzl.'"
27. Yitzhak Teutsch, *The Cyprus Detention Camps: The Essential Research Guide* (Newcastle upon Tyne: Cambridge Scholars Publishing, 2019), 84; Palmach Association, "Guardian — Herzl"; Ruth Gruber, *Witness: One of the Great Foreign Correspondents of the Twentieth Century Tells Her Story* (New York: Shocken Books, 2009), 117.
28. Teutsch, *The Cyprus Detention Camps*, 84.
29. Ibid., 20.
30. Jason Steinhauer, "Retracing the Steps of Refugees on Cyprus," Library of Congress, November 23, 2015, https://blogs.loc.gov/kluge/2015/11/retracing-the-

steps-of-refugees-on-cyprus/; Gregory Katz, "The Illegal Immigration," Dpcamps.org, accessed September 14, 2020, http://www.dpcamps.org/illegalimmigration.html.
31. Steinhauer, "Retracing the Steps of Refugees on Cyprus"; Katz, "The Illegal Immigration."
32. Steinhauer, "Retracing the Steps of Refugees on Cyprus."
33. Teutsch, *The Cyprus Detention Camps*, 20.
34. Ibid., 338; Steinhauer, "Retracing the Steps of Refugees on Cyprus."
35. Gruber, *Witness*, 119.
36. "Cyprus Detention Camps," Holocaust Encyclopedia, United States Holocaust Memorial Museum, accessed April 30, 2021, https://encyclopedia.ushmm.org/content/en/article/cyprus-detention-camps.
37. "Cyprus Detention Camps," Yad Vashem, accessed April 30, 2021, https://www.yadvashem.org/odot_pdf/Microsoft%20Word%20-%20727.pdf.
38. Gruber, *Witness*, 119.
39. Teutsch, *The Cyprus Detention Camps*, 338.
40. Yad Vashem, "Cyprus Detention Camps."
41. Ibid.
42. Ibid.; Steinhauer, "Retracing the Steps of Refugees on Cyprus."
43. United States Holocaust Memorial Museum, "Cyprus Detention Camps."
44. Meron Medzini, *Golda Meir: A Political Biography* (Tel Aviv: De Gruyter Oldenbourg, 2008), 129–30.
45. Ibid., 131–32.
46. "Israeli Society & Culture: Jewish Agency for Israel (JAFI)," Jewish Virtual Library, accessed September 13, 2020, https://www.jewishvirtuallibrary.org/jewish-agency-for-israel-jafi.
47. Gruber, *Witness*, 120; Medzini, *Golda Meir*, 132.
48. Medzini, *Golda Meir*, 132.
49. Gruber, *Witness*, 120; Ruth Gruber, *Raquela: A Woman of Israel* (New York: Open Road Media, 2014), 188.
50. Yad Vashem, "Cyprus Detention Camps."
51. Gruber, *Witness*, 119–20.
52. Gruber, *Raquela*, 188.
53. Ibid.; Medzini, *Golda Meir*, 132.
54. Gruber, *Raquela*, 189; Gruber, *Witness*, 120.
55. Gruber, *Witness*, 120.
56. Ibid.
57. Ibid.
58. "Learning More about the Children of Cyprus," JDC Archives, accessed April 30, 2021, https://archives.jdc.org/learning-more-about-the-children-of-cyprus/.
59. Tessler, *A History of the Israeli-Palestinian Conflict*, 258–61.
60. Ibid.

Chapter 21

1. Natalie Walker, "The Displaced Persons Act of 1948," Truman Library Institute, April 29, 2019, https://www.trumanlibraryinstitute.org/the-displaced-persons-act-of-1948/.
2. Ibid.

Chapter 22

1. "549 Weary D.P.'s Land Here," *Boston Daily Globe*, January 18, 1949, 1, 7.
2. Andy Kessler, "The Story of the S.S. Marine Flasher," thekesslers.com, accessed September 15, 2020, http://thekesslers.com/family/tibor/Marine_Flasher.html.
3. Ibid.
4. Boston Daily Globe, "549 Weary D.P.'s Land Here."
5. Ibid.
6. Ibid.
7. Ibid.

Chapter 24

1. "Vandals Damage Jewish Center in Queens; Tear Total Scrolls Section," *JTA Daily News Bulletin*, June 22, 1965, 6, http://pdfs.jta.org/1965/1965-06-22_119.pdf?_ga=2.104326723.2140151901.1600134794-1880556188.1599531396.
2. Ibid.

Chapter 25

1. Dana Evan Kaplan, "Fleeing the Revolution: The Exodus of Cuban Jewry in the Early 1960s," *Cuban Studies* 36, no. 1 (2005): 130-133, https://doi.org/10.1353/cub.2005.0036.
2. Caren Osten Gerszberg, "In Cuba, Finding a Tiny Corner of Jewish Life," *New York Times*, February 4, 2007, https://www.nytimes.com/2007/02/04/travel/04journeys.html.

Chapter 28

1. Irene Newhouse, trans., "Mistrial," July 11, 1968, https://kehilalinks.jewishgen.org/lida-district/winwer-mistrial.htm.
2. Irene Newhouse, trans., "The Indictment Against Leopold Windisch and Rudolf Werner for War Crimes, Significant Findings: Political Biography

(Windisch)," December 15, 1968, https://kehilalinks.jewishgen.org/lida-district/winwer7.htm.
3. Irene Newhouse, trans., "The Indictment Against Leopold Windisch and Rudolf Werner for War Crimes, The Crimes – Windisch," December 15, 1968, https://kehilalinks.jewishgen.org/lida-district/winwer22.htm#Ivje%20(12%20May.
4. Irene Newhouse, trans., "The Indictment Against Leopold Windisch and Rudolf Werner for War Crimes, Significant Findings: Political Biography (Werner)," December 15, 1968, https://kehilalinks.jewishgen.org/lida-district/winwer12.htm.
5. Irene Newhouse, trans., "The Indictment Against Leopold Windisch and Rudolf Werner for War Crimes, The Crimes – Werner," December 15, 1968, https://kehilalinks.jewishgen.org/lida-district/winwer23.htm#Ivje.
6. Irene Newhouse, trans., "Significant Findings Political Biography (Werner)."
7. Irene Newhouse, trans., "The Indictment Against Leopold Windisch and Rudolf Werner for War Crimes, Significant Findings: Austrian Legal Proceedings Against the Accused for the Same Deeds (Windisch)," December 15, 1968, https://kehilalinks.jewishgen.org/lida-district/winwer10.htm.
8. "Laute Leitung," *Der Spiegel*, June 1, 1969, https://www.spiegel.de/spiegel/print/d-45741013.html.
9. Irene Newhouse, trans., "Trial 2," February 12, 1969, https://kehilalinks.jewishgen.org/lida-district/winwer-trial2.htm.
10. Irene Newhouse, trans., "Trial History and Verdict," accessed May 1, 2021, https://kehilalinks.jewishgen.org/lida-district/winwer-verdict.htm.
11. Ibid.
12. Ibid.
13. Ibid.
14. Ibid.
15. David Fraser, *Daviborshch's Cart: Narrating the Holocaust in Australian War Crimes Trials* (Lincoln: University of Nebraska Press, 2011), 97.
16. Peggy O'Donnell, "'Gateway to Hell': A Nazi Mass Grave, Forensic Scientists, and an Australian War Crimes Trial," *Holocaust and Genocide Studies* 32, no. 3 (Winter 2018): 365, https://doi.org/10.1093/hgs/dcy060.
17. Ibid., 363.
18. Ibid., 361.
19. Ibid.
20. Fraser, *Daviborshch's Cart*, 98.
21. Ibid., 98–99.
22. O'Donnell, *Gateway to Hell*, 362.
23. Ibid.
24. Ibid., 370.
25. Ibid.
26. Ibid., 370–72.
27. Ibid., 371.
28. Ibid., 370.
29. Ibid., 361, 372; Fraser, *Daviborshch's Cart*, 95; Daniel Keane, "Ivan Polyukhovich: How an Alleged Nazi War Criminal was Acquitted by an Australian Court,"

ABC News, May 19, 2018, https://www.abc.net.au/news/2018-05-20/nazi-war-criminals-in-australia-and-the-case-of-polyukhovich/9756454.

30. O'Donnell, *Gateway to Hell*, 373–74.
31. Ibid., 374.
32. Michael Machosky, "11 Killed in Pittsburgh Synagogue Massacre; Gunman Yelled 'All Jews Must Die'" *Times of Israel*, October 27, 2018, https://www.timesofisrael.com/at-least-11-killed-in-pittsburgh-synagogue-shooting/.
33. Campbell Robertson, Christopher Mele, and Sabrina Tavernise, "11 Killed in Synagogue Massacre; Suspect Charged With 29 Counts," *New York Times*, October 27, 2018, https://www.nytimes.com/2018/10/27/us/active-shooter-pittsburgh-synagogue-shooting.html.
34. Miriam Jordan, "HIAS, the Jewish Agency Criticized by the Shooting Suspect, Has a History of Aiding Refugees," *New York Times*, October 28, 2018, https://www.nytimes.com/2018/10/28/us/hias-pittsburgh-robert-bowers.html.
35. "Marine Flasher Docks with Several Hundred Refugees; Aided by HIAS, JDC, USNA," *JTA Daily News Bulletin*, November 11, 1947, 6, http://pdfs.jta.org/1947/1947-11-11_262.pdf?_ga=2.136059313.1293895354.1600224985-1880556188.1599531396.
36. Jacob Eder, "Why HIAS Became a Target of Hate," *Atlantic*, October 28, 2018, https://www.theatlantic.com/ideas/archive/2018/10/what-is-hiasand-why-did-the-pittsburgh-gunman-target-its-work/574204/.
37. Farnoush Amiri, "Accused Pittsburgh Gunman Posted Online about HIAS, an Agency Known for Work with Refugees," *NBC News*, October 28, 2018, https://www.nbcnews.com/news/crime-courts/pittsburgh-shooting-suspect-posted-online-about-hias-agency-known-work-n925391.
38. "HIAS Calls Trump Administration's Proposed Refugee Ceiling Shameful," HIAS, September 17, 2018, https://www.hias.org/news/press-releases/hias-calls-trump-administrations-proposed-refugee-ceiling-shameful.
39. "HIAS, ADL Oppose Administration Changes to Asylum Laws," HIAS, July 15, 2020, https://www.hias.org/news/press-releases/hias-adl-oppose-administration-changes-asylum-laws.
40. Sharon Samber, "Still Fighting the Muslim Ban After Two Years," HIAS, January 26, 2019, https://www.hias.org/blog/still-fighting-muslim-ban-after-two-years.
41. Emma Green, "The Fight to Make Meaning Out of a Massacre," *Atlantic*, September 29, 2019, https://www.theatlantic.com/politics/archive/2019/09/pittsburgh-politics-violence-gun-reform/598885/.
42. American & International Societies for Yad Vashem, "The Changing Image of Holocaust Victims," *Martyrdom & Resistance* 40, no. 4 (March/April 2014): 1, https://www.yadvashemusa.org/wp-content/uploads/2017/03/2014_march_april.pdf.
43. Ibid.
44. Ibid.

Epilogue

1. "Lessons Learned," *Stories I Tell Myself* (blog), February 22, 2021, https://stories-i-tell-myself.com/2021/02/22/lessons-learned/.
2. "About Us," USC Shoah Foundation, accessed September 17, 2020, https://sfi.usc.edu/about.
3. Paula Bakst, interview by Harriette Kanew, *Visual History Archive Online*, USC Shoah Foundation, August 17, 1995, Tape 6, 10:37.
4. David Bakst, interview by Scott Fried, *Visual History Archive Online*, USC Shoah Foundation, August 17, 1995, Tape 4, 25:49.

ACKNOWLEDGMENTS

As miraculous as this story is, it is also one of great trauma. I am thankful to the many family members and friends who not only dedicated significant amounts of time to speak with me, but also relived painful memories in the process. These include Moshe Baran and Allen Small, dear friends of my grandparents who each have their own remarkable stories of survival; Ben Feder and Rochelle Stern, whom I am grateful to for teaching me about their inspirational mother; my parents, aunts, and uncle—Shari Bakst, Steven Bakst, Rochelle Bakst, Doreen Fleischman, Linda Bakst, and Gary Bakst—who shared stories, answered many questions, and helped locate pictures and documents. I am further grateful to my parents and Uncle Gary for their helpful feedback on earlier versions of the manuscript.

For as long as they were able, Bubby and Poppy were open about their lives with me. As I was drafting this book, Poppy fielded copious phone calls, graciously answering my numerous and often unpleasant questions even as his health waned. In the process, Bubby and Poppy gave me the priceless gift of getting to know my ancestors and instilling in me some of their resilience, strength, and tenacity. Bubby and Poppy were the most loving and devoted grandparents a kid could have. Being their granddaughter will always be what I am most proud of.

Finally, I am particularly appreciative of my father, Steven Bakst, who spent countless hours helping me write this book. His encouragement, ideas, and stories are the reason *The Shoemaker's Son* was written.

AMSTERDAM PUBLISHERS HOLOCAUST LIBRARY

The series **Holocaust Survivor Memoirs World War II** consists of the following autobiographies of survivors:

Outcry. Holocaust Memoirs, by Manny Steinberg

Hank Brodt Holocaust Memoirs. A Candle and a Promise, by Deborah Donnelly

The Dead Years. Holocaust Memoirs, by Joseph Schupack

Rescued from the Ashes. The Diary of Leokadia Schmidt, Survivor of the Warsaw Ghetto, by Leokadia Schmidt

My Lvov. Holocaust Memoir of a twelve-year-old Girl, by Janina Hescheles

Remembering Ravensbrück. From Holocaust to Healing, by Natalie Hess

Wolf. A Story of Hate, by Zeev Scheinwald with Ella Scheinwald

Save my Children. An Astonishing Tale of Survival and its Unlikely Hero, by Leon Kleiner with Edwin Stepp

Holocaust Memoirs of a Bergen-Belsen Survivor & Classmate of Anne Frank, by Nanette Blitz Konig

Defiant German - Defiant Jew. A Holocaust Memoir from inside the Third Reich, by Walter Leopold with Les Leopold

In a Land of Forest and Darkness. The Holocaust Story of two Jewish Partisans, by Sara Lustigman Omelinski

Holocaust Memories. Annihilation and Survival in Slovakia, by Paul Davidovits

From Auschwitz with Love. The Inspiring Memoir of Two Sisters' Survival, Devotion and Triumph Told by Manci Grunberger Beran & Ruth Grunberger Mermelstein, by Daniel Seymour

Remetz. Resistance Fighter and Survivor of the Warsaw Ghetto, by Jan Yohay Remetz

My March Through Hell. A Young Girl's Terrifying Journey to Survival, by Halina Kleiner with Edwin Stepp

Roman's Journey, by Roman Halter

Beyond Borders. Escaping the Holocaust and Fighting the Nazis. 1938-1948, by Rudi Haymann

The Engineers. A memoir of survival through World War II in Poland and Hungary, by Henry Reiss

Memoirs by Elmar Rivosh, Sculptor (1906-1967). Riga Ghetto and Beyond, by Elmar Rivosh

The series **Holocaust Survivor True Stories** consists of the following biographies:

Among the Reeds. The true story of how a family survived the Holocaust, by Tammy Bottner

A Holocaust Memoir of Love & Resilience. Mama's Survival from Lithuania to America, by Ettie Zilber

Living among the Dead. My Grandmother's Holocaust Survival Story of Love and Strength, by Adena Bernstein Astrowsky

Heart Songs. A Holocaust Memoir, by Barbara Gilford

Shoes of the Shoah. The Tomorrow of Yesterday, by Dorothy Pierce

Hidden in Berlin. A Holocaust Memoir, by Evelyn Joseph Grossman

Separated Together. The Incredible True WWII Story of Soulmates Stranded an Ocean Apart, by Kenneth P. Price, Ph.D.

The Man Across the River. The incredible story of one man's will to survive the Holocaust, by Zvi Wiesenfeld

If Anyone Calls, Tell Them I Died. A Memoir, by Emanuel (Manu) Rosen

The House on Thrömerstrasse. A Story of Rebirth and Renewal in the Wake of the Holocaust, by Ron Vincent

Dancing with my Father. His hidden past. Her quest for truth. How Nazi Vienna shaped a family's identity, by Jo Sorochinsky

The Story Keeper. Weaving the Threads of Time and Memory - A Memoir, by Fred Feldman

Krisia's Silence. The Girl who was not on Schindler's List, by Ronny Hein

Defying Death on the Danube. A Holocaust Survival Story, by Debbie J. Callahan with Henry Stern

A Doorway to Heroism. A decorated German-Jewish Soldier who became an American Hero, by Rabbi W. Jack Romberg

The Shoemaker's Son. The Life of a Holocaust Resister, by Laura Beth Bakst

The Redhead of Auschwitz. A True Story, by Nechama Birnbaum

Land of Many Bridges. My Father's Story, by Bela Ruth Samuel Tenenholtz

Creating Beauty from the Abyss. The Amazing Story of Sam Herciger, Auschwitz Survivor and Artist, by Lesley Ann Richardson

On Sunny Days We Sang. A Holocaust Story of Survival and Resilience, by Jeannette Grunhaus de Gelman

Painful Joy. A Holocaust Family Memoir, by Max J. Friedman

I Give You My Heart. A True Story of Courage and Survival, by Wendy Holden

In the Time of Madmen, by Mark A. Prelas

Monsters and Miracles. Horror, Heroes and the Holocaust, by Ira Wesley Kitmacher

Flower of Vlora. Growing up Jewish in Communist Albania, by Anna Kohen

Aftermath: Coming of Age on Three Continents. A Memoir, by Annette Libeskind Berkovits

Not a real Enemy. The True Story of a Hungarian Jewish Man's Fight for Freedom, by Robert Wolf

Zaidy's War. Four Armies, Three Continents, Two Brothers. One Man's Impossible Story of Endurance, by Martin Bodek

The Glassmaker's Son. Looking for the World my Father left behind in Nazi Germany, by Peter Kupfer

The Apprentice of Buchenwald. The True Story of the Teenage Boy Who Sabotaged Hitler's War Machine, by Oren Schneider

Good for a Single Journey, by Helen Joyce

Burying the Ghosts. She escaped Nazi Germany only to have her life torn apart by the woman she saved from the camps: her mother, by Sonia Case

American Wolf. From Nazi Refugee to American Spy. A True Story, by Audrey Birnbaum

Bipolar Refugee. A Saga of Survival and Resilience, by Peter Wiesner

Before the Beginning and After the End, by Hymie Anisman

Malka Owsiany recounts, by Mark Turkow (editor)

I Will Give Them an Everlasting Name. Jacksonville's Stories of the Holocaust, by Samuel P. Cox

www.ingramcontent.com/pod-product-compliance
Lightning Source LLC
LaVergne TN
LVHW041915070526
838199LV00051BA/2626